Instant Revit!:
Commercial Drawing Using Autodesk® Revit® 2015

By: David Martin

Autodesk®, AutoCAD®, DWG®, the DWG® logo, and Inventor® are registered trademarks or trademarks of Autodesk®, Inc., and/or its
subsidiaries and/or affiliates in the USA and other countries.

Autodesk® screen shots reprinted with the permission of Autodesk®, Inc. Autodesk®, the Autodesk® logo, and Revit®, are registered
trademarks or trademarks of Autodesk®, Inc., and/or its subsidiaries and/or affiliates in the USA and/or other countries.

The information contained in the book and website including webpages, book samples, video files, and other information is not meant to
substitute for design advice from a Licensed Architect, Structural Engineer, or Designer for purposes of building construction. The project in
this book and the associated drawings were created using generally accepted design practice but have not been verified to be compliant with
international or local building codes. The models, images, and construction documents produced from the use of the textbook and videos
tutorials are not approved for construction.

Dedication

I would like to dedicate this book to my friends and co-workers. Without their constant support and friendship this book would not be possible.

Table of Contents

Introduction

Welcome to: **Commercial Drawing Using Autodesk® Revit® 2015.**

The purpose of this book is to guide the student through the process of drawing a one-story commercial building. This project was originally designed using the Revit 2014 program and has been updated for the 2015 version.

Please Note:
This project is meant for students that have a basic understanding of Revit. If you have never used Revit before, you may wish to first purchase my other book: **Instant Revit!: A Quick and Easy Guide to Learning Autodesk® Revit ® 2015.** This book goes into much more depth and covers the basic commands and techniques of the Revit 2015 software.

As you work your way through this project, please refer to the support files on the Instant Revit! website at www.instantrevit.com. There are many files that you will find useful and will help you complete the project. The website also contains a link to videos that show a demonstration of each tutorial from the beginning to the end of the project.

This project was originally developed for my Introduction to Revit course at Glendale Community College in Glendale, California and I continue to use this book for my students.

Each of the eight tutorials is divided into parts that will have the student accomplish a portion of the project. On the next few pages is a listing of the tutorials and their individual parts. In order to save your progress through the tutorials, it is recommended that you save at the completion of each part of the tutorial. You may refer to the PDF portfolio on the companion website for the finished version of the project.

It is my hope that you find the process of completing the project an enjoyable and valuable experience. Once you have completed the book please feel free to email me or fill out the on-line forms on the website to share your experiences, suggestions, and compliments.

Enjoy,

David Martin
instantrevit@gmail.com
www.instantrevit.com

Commercial Project Tutorials

Tutorial 1 – Creating the Commercial Building Layout		
Part 1	Adding the Grids and Levels
Part 2	Modifying and Adding the Exterior and Interior Walls
Part 3	Modifying the Door Tag, Tagging the Doors and Windows, and Dimensioning
Part 4	Modifying the Exterior Walls
Part 5	Creating the Footers, Floor Slab, and Longitudinal Section
Part 6	Creating the Roof and Roof Symbols
Part 7	Adding the Tower Walls and Roof

Starting the Tutorial

1. Before starting the Revit program, create a file structure on your flash drive or hard drive to store your files.
   - Create a folder called Commercial Project. You will store your drawings in this folder.
   - Open the folder and create three subfolders called Families, Image Files, and PDF Files.
2. Download the Custom Family files from the Instant Revit website at **www.instantrevit.com**.
3. The families are located under the Support Files page. Extract the zip file or download the families to your Families folder on your local drive.
4. Create a new drawing file. Use the Commercial-Default.rte file for the template.
5. Name the file CL1-1.
6. Open the file.

Note:
As you complete each tutorial it is recommended to save the file with the Tutorial Number and Part Number in the file name (i.e. CL1-1 = Commercial Lesson Tutorial 1, Part 1.).

CL1-1 - Adding the Grids and Levels

1. Open the Level 1 View.
2. Begin by placing grids on the drawing. The Grid command is in the Architecture Ribbon, Datum Panel. These will be used to locate the walls. Refer to the dimensions for the locations.
3. To change the Grid letter/number, click on the grid line and then the bubble. Type in the correct letter or number.

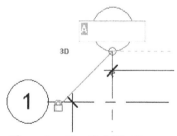

Changing the Grid Letter

4. To turn on/off the grid bubble click on the line and the click inside the checkbox.

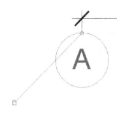

Hide/Show Grid Bubble Checkbox

5. Your grid layout should look like this when finished…

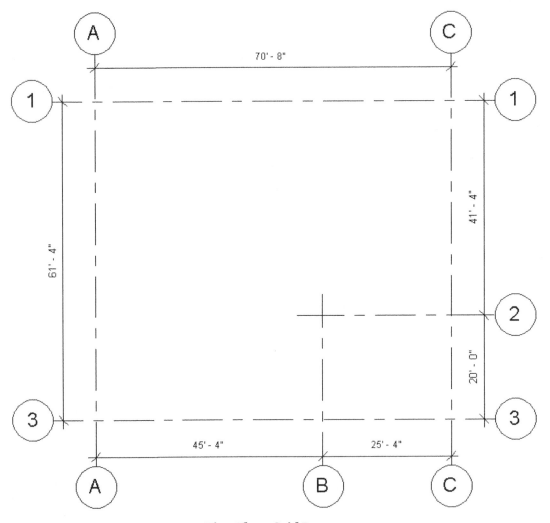

First Floor Grid Layout

6. Go to the South Elevation view. Create the levels at these heights. Delete any extra levels that will not be used.

7. You may either copy an existing level using the copy tool or create a new level using the Level tool in the Architecture tab, Datum panel.

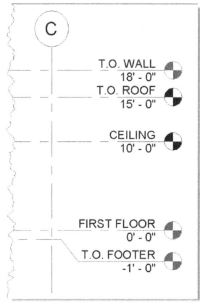

Levels Needed for Project

8. Create a view for T.O. Roof. Go to the Plan Views tool in the View tab, Create panel.

9. Select Floor Plan.

Floor Plan Selected

10. In the New Floor Plan dialog box, select T.O. ROOF. A new floor plan view will appear in the Project Browser.

T.O. Roof Selected

11. This is the end of Part 1. Save your file as CL1-1.

CL1-2 - Modifying and Adding the Exterior and Interior Walls

1. Continuing from the CL1-1 file, save the file and then save the file as CL1-2.

2. Open the First Floor View.

3. Create a new wall style called Exterior – Concrete on Mtl. Stud. Use this setup for the walls. When creating the wall type, start with the Generic 8" type.

   This wall will consist of an 8" Cast-In-Place Concrete wall with a Moisture Barrier, Metal Furring, and Gypsum Wall Board.

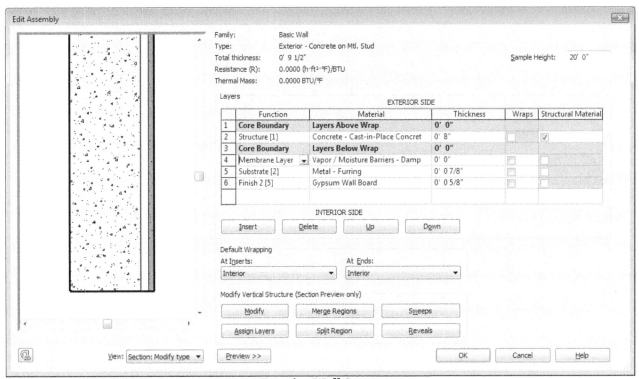

Exterior Wall Setup

4. Add the exterior walls to the drawing.

5. Use the Align tool in the Modify tab, Modify panel to lock the walls to the grid lines.

   Draw the walls in a clockwise direction so that the exterior side of the wall is facing outward. You can check which side is facing outward by selecting the wall and observing which side the flip arrows are. The arrows are on the outside of the wall.

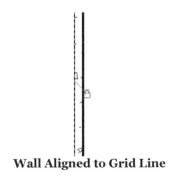

Wall Aligned to Grid Line

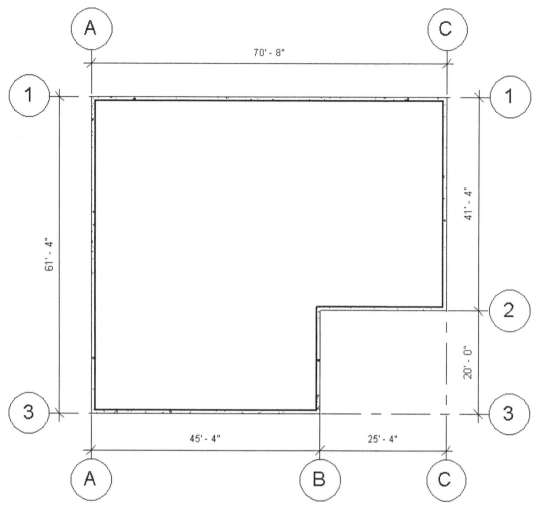

Exterior Walls Added

6. Add the interior walls.

   - Refer to the diagram for the location of the walls.

   - Use the "Basic Wall – Interior – 5 1/2" Partition (1-Hr)" style for all interior walls.

   - The exception is the wall that separates the Office from the Storage. For this wall use "Basic Wall – Interior – 4 7/8" Partition (1-Hr)".

   - Set the height of the walls to the Ceiling Level and the Top Offset to 2'-0". This will give the wall a total height of 12'-0".

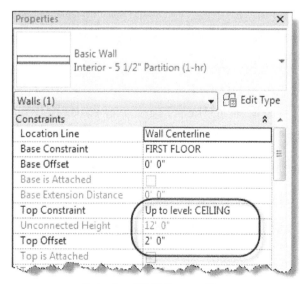

Interior Wall Properties

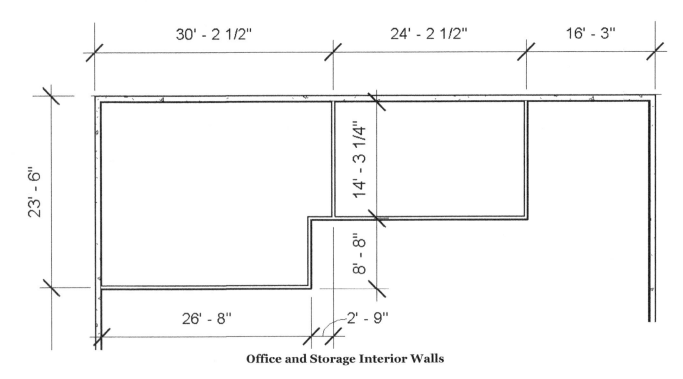

Office and Storage Interior Walls

7. Next, add the restroom walls.
   - Use Basic Wall – Interior – 4 7/8" Partition (1-Hr) for these walls.
   - These walls will be also be set to the Ceiling level height plus 2'-0" (12'-0").

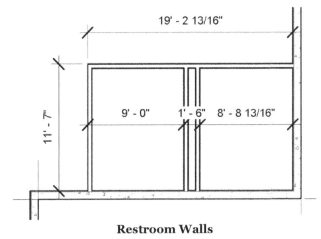

Restroom Walls

8. Add the Doors and Windows.
   - Refer to the schedules for sizes.
   - The locations are given on the next page.
   - The main entrance Curtain Wall Dbl Glass door and south wall windows will be added later.
   - The tags for the doors and windows are for reference. You will add these tags later in the tutorial.

DOOR SCHEDULE				
MARK	WIDTH	HEIGHT	THICK.	TYPE
A	5' - 9 1/2"	6' - 10 3/4"	0' - 0 1/4"	Curtain Wall Dbl Glass
B	3' - 0"	6' - 8"	0' - 2"	36" x 80"
C	3' - 0"	7' - 0"	0' - 2"	36" x 84"

WINDOW SCHEDULE			
MARK	WIDTH	HEIGHT	TYPE
1	3' - 0"	4' - 0"	Fixed: 36" x 48"
2	3' - 0"	6' - 0"	Fixed: 36" x 72"
3	4' - 0"	6' - 0"	Fixed: 48" x 72"
4	4' - 0"	3' - 0"	Fixed: 48" x 36"

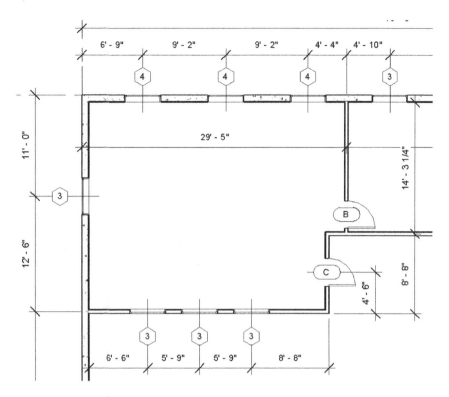

Office Area Door and Window Locations

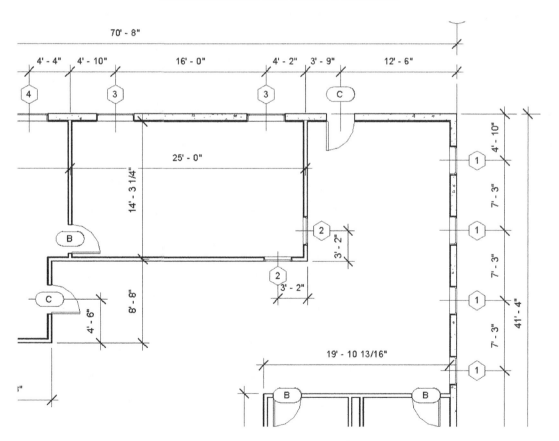

Storage Room and Northeast Wall Door and Window Locations

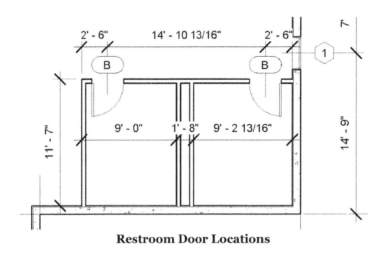

Restroom Door Locations

9. This is the end of Part 2. Save your file as CL1-2.

CL1-3 - Tagging and Dimensioning the Doors and Windows

1. Continuing from the CL1-2 file, save the file and then save the file as CL1-3.

2. Before tagging the doors and windows you will need to modify the tags so that the numbers/letters will show up with the correct format. You will also need to create a masking region so that the extension lines are broken when they cross over the tags.

3. You will begin by modifying the door tags.
   - Go to the Door Tag family in the Project Browser.
   - It is located in the Families Category, Annotation Symbols sub-category, Door Tag family.

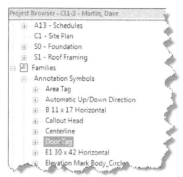

Door Tag Family in Project Browser

4. Right click on the Door tag family and select Edit. This will open the family file (Door Tag.rfa).

5. You will need to change the Door Tag family so that the number/letter is based on the type mark and not the mark.

6. Click on the field for the mark. This is the text labeled 101.

7. The text will turn blue. Click on the Edit... button next to Label in the Properties Box.

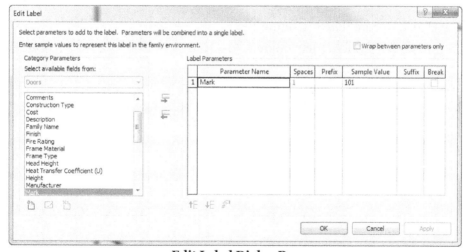

Edit Label Dialog Box

8. In the Edit Label dialog box click on the 1 next to the Mark in the Parameter Name field.

9. Click the red arrow to remove the parameter.

10. In the Category Parameters area, scroll down to Type Mark. Click the green arrow to add the parameter.

11. Click OK.

12. The text in the bubble has changed to 1t.

Adding the Masking Region

1. Click on the Masking Region tool in the Create tab, Detail panel.

Masking Region Tool

2. Select the Pick Lines option in the Draw panel.

Pick Lines Option

3. Click on the two arcs and two lines the make up the boundary of the symbol.

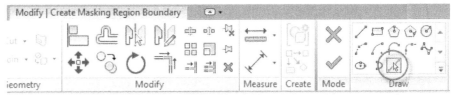

Boundary Picked

4. Click the Green Check to complete the boundary.

5. Click the Load into Project tool in the ribbon to load the Door Tag into the project.

6. Select "Overwrite the existing version" to replace the original door tag.

   (This will only affect this drawing.)

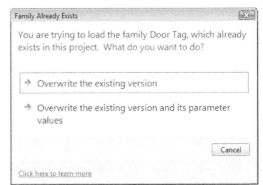

Family Already Exists Box

7. Repeat the process for the window tag. You will not need to change the label, only add the masking region.

8. Tag and dimension the door and window locations. Refer to the diagram for the location of the tags.

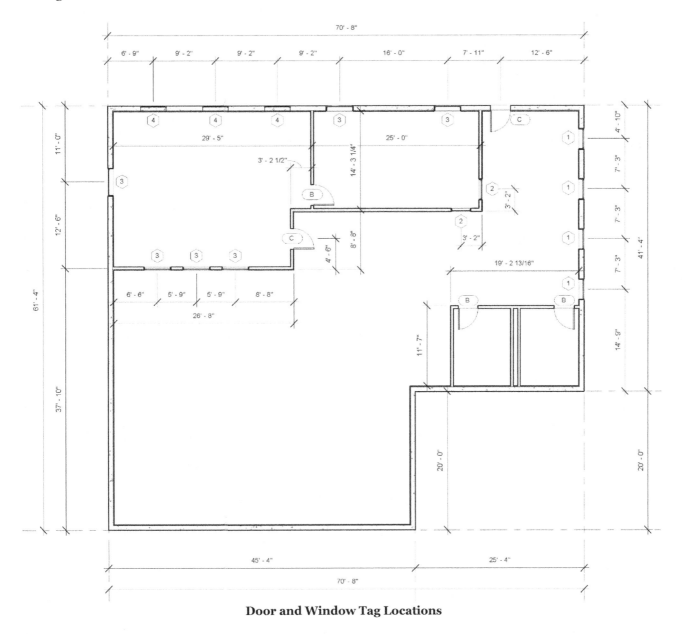

Door and Window Tag Locations

9. This is the end of Part 3. Save your file as CL1-3.

CL1-4 - Modifying the Exterior Walls

1. Continuing from the CL1-3 file, save the file and then save the file as CL1-4.

2. Select the Exterior Walls in the First Floor view.

3. The bottom constraint of the wall needs to be changed. Currently the wall has a base constraint of FIRST FLOOR. Select all of the exterior walls and change the base constraint to T.O. FOOTER.

4. Change top of the wall to T.O. WALL. The total height should be 19'-0".

5. Edit the structure of the wall.
   - Open the Edit Assembly dialog box for the wall.
   - Switch to the Section view of the wall and zoom in to the top of the wall.
   - Click on the Modify button in the Modify Vertical Structure area of the dialog box.
   - Click on the line as indicated by the arrows.
   - Unlock the Metal Furring and Gypsum Board layers.
   - Repeat the process for the layers at the bottom of the wall.

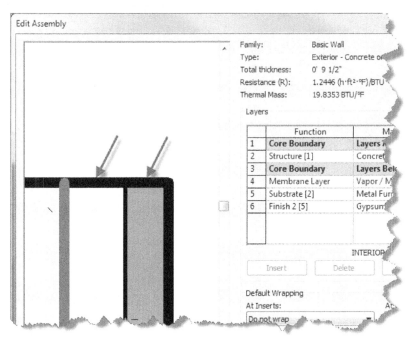

**Unlock Top and Bottom Ends of Layers
(Top Portion Shown)**

6. Select the wall and match the settings to the properties shown.

   Note:
   The reason for the Top Extension Distance -7'-0" setting is so that the drywall will be below the bottom edge of the roof and above the Ceiling.

Settings for Exterior Walls

7. Switch to the 3D view and set the view to Shaded. Your view should look like this...

    Note:
    The shadows have been switched on for clarity. You can do this by clicking on the Shadows On toggle at the bottom of the view window.

Shadows On Toggle

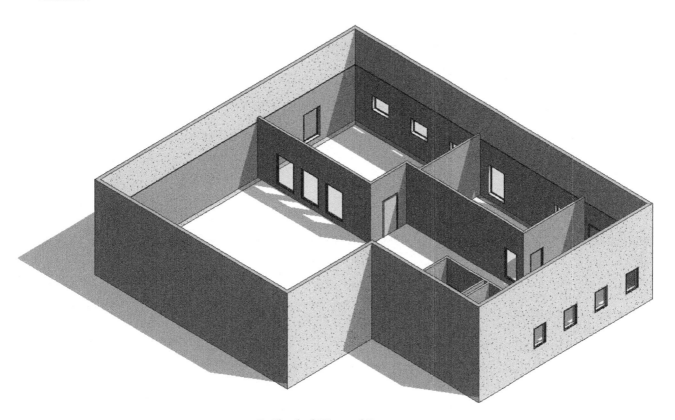

3D Shaded View of Structure

8. This is the end of Part 4. Save your file as CL1-4.

CL1-5 - Creating the Footers, Floor Slab, and Longitudinal Section

1. Continuing from the CL1-4 file, save the file and then save the file as CL1-5.

2. Go to the T.O. Footer view.

3. Create new foundation wall type 1'-4" wide. Name the type Foundation – 1'-4" Wide.

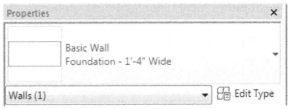

Foundation Wall Type

4. Set the View Range for the view so that the bottom and the view depth offsets are at -1'-0".
   This way you will be able to see the foundation wall as it is placed.

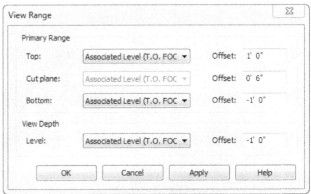

View Range Settings

5. Place the foundation wall centered on the concrete exterior wall. Use the following settings for the wall properties.
   - When placing the foundation wall, use the Core Centerline for the center of the wall.
   - This way the foundation wall will be centered on the concrete portion of the exterior wall.

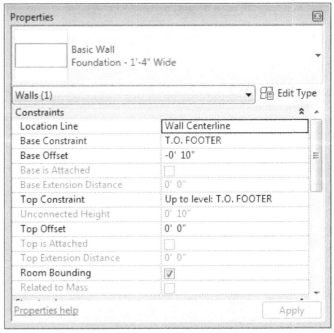

Foundation Wall Properties

6. Zoom in on the lower left corner.
   - Note that the footer is centered on the concrete portion of the wall.
   - The metal stud and gypsum board layers are not visible due to the cut plane settings.

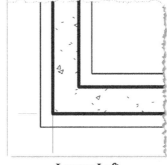

Lower Left

7. Open the First Floor view.

8. Create the floor slab. Start with the 4" Concrete Slab and duplicate. Name the floor type "Slab on Grade – 4" w/Carpet.

9. When placing the boundary, pick the inside face of the concrete - not the edge of the drywall furring.
   Refer to the diagrams below.

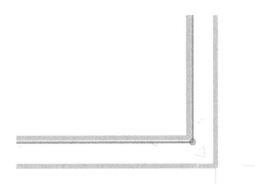

Floor Sketch Boundary

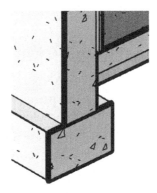

3D View of Footer, Slab, and Wall

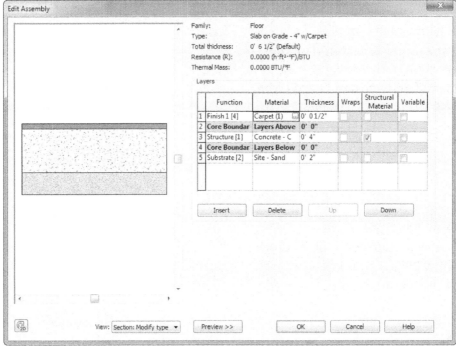

Slab Settings

Creating the Longitudinal Section

1. Open the First Floor Plan view.

2. Go to the View tab, Create panel, Section tool. Left-click on the tool. In the type selector make sure the Building Section type is selected.

3. Click on the left side of the floor plan for the start point. Drag to the right and click on the other side of the floor plan for the second point.

4. Click on the break control symbol in the middle of the cutting plane line to break it. You can adjust the length of the line by dragging the handle point.

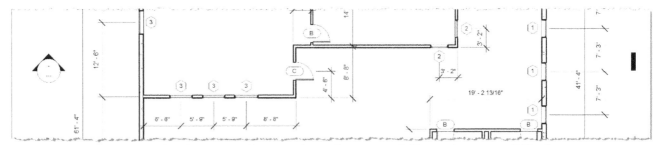

Longitudinal Section Line Location (The tags and dimensions may differ.)

5. Open the view named Section 1 and rename the view Longitudinal Section.

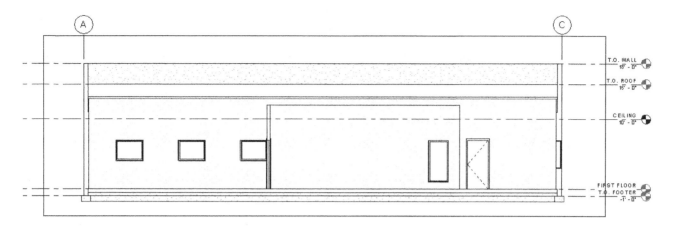

Longitudinal Section View

6. You will need to adjust the crop window of the window to match the example.
7. The scale of the view is 3/16"=1'-0".
8. This is the end of Part 5. Save your file as CL1-5.

CL1-6 - Creating the Roof and Roof Symbols

1. Continuing from the CL1-5 file, save the file and then save the file again as CL1-6.
2. Open the Roof Plan view.
3. Click on the Roof tool in the Architecture tab, Build panel.
4. Select the Insulation on Metal Deck – EPDM roof type.
5. Click on the Edit Type button.
6. Duplicate the type and rename it Steel Truss – Insulation on Metal Deck – EPDM.
7. Modify the structure. Refer to the picture below for specifications.
8. Click the OK button twice to complete the process.

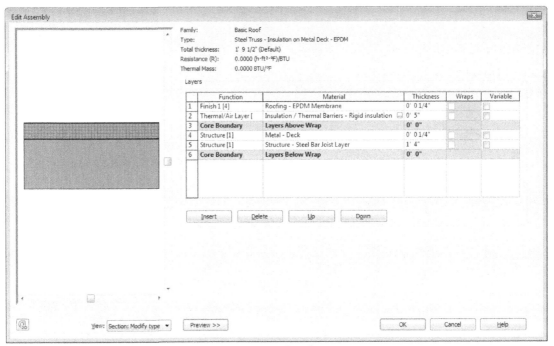

New Roof Style

9. Begin the process of adding the roof by selecting the Base Level of the roof.
10. Open the T.O. ROOF view.
11. Click on the Roof tool in the Architecture tab, Build panel.
12. Select the Pick Walls option in the Draw panel.
13. Set the Base Offset from Level to -1' 9 1/2". (This is equal to the thickness of the roof.)

14. Select the inside of the walls for the roof boundary. After picking the walls, you will need to move the magenta edge to the edge of the concrete portion of the wall.

Before   **After**

15. When finished with the boundary click the Green Check.

16. This is the end of Part 6. Save your file as CL1-6.

CL1-7 - Adding the Tower Walls and Roof

Now that you have completed the exterior walls of the structure, the next thing to include in the project is a tower around the front entry area.

You will begin by adding four walls around the front entry. You will also add two additional walls stacked on top of the two exterior walls at the bottom right corner of the building.

1. Continuing from the CL1-6 file, save the file and then save the file again as CL1-7.

2. Open the First Floor view.

3. Create a new wall type called Exterior – Stucco on Metal Stud. Begin with the Generic – 8" wall type.
   - Refer to the diagram below for layer materials and sizes.

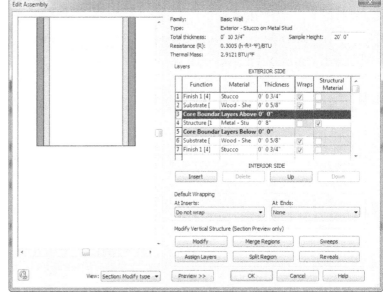

Tower Wall Settings

4. Add the walls to the lower right corner of the building. Align the inside edges to the corner of the existing exterior walls.
   - Set the height of the walls to T.O. WALL.

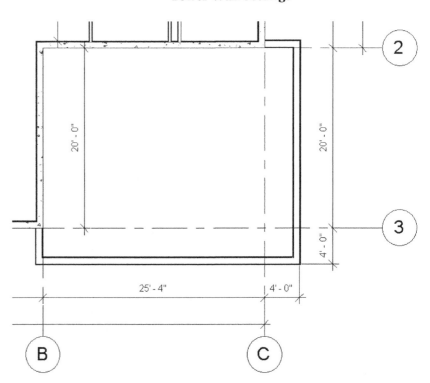

Tower Wall Location

5. Switch to the south elevation view.

6. Add a new level called: T.O. TOWER. Set the height to 22'-0".

7. Switch back to the First Floor view. Select the four tower walls and change the top constraint to T.O. TOWER.

8. This is what you should have so far...

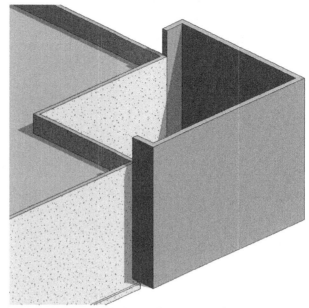

3D View of Tower Walls

9. Switch to the T.O WALL view.
   - If you do not have the view, go to the Plan Views tool in the View Menu, Create Panel.
   - Select the Floor Plan option and choose the T.O. WALL level.

10. Next you will add two walls to enclose the tower portion. Use the same wall type as the tower walls.

11. When placing the walls, align the walls with the face with the outer face of the exterior wall.
   - Set the Bottom Constraint to T.O. WALL and the Top Constraint to T.O. TOWER.
   - This will create an overhang where the bottom of the wall meets the top of the concrete wall.

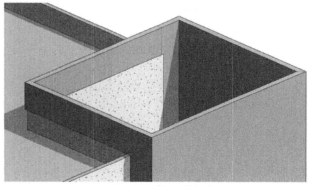

Two Walls Added

Creating the Openings in the Tower Walls

To complete the tower walls you will add two large openings to the walls. This will allow foot traffic to pass through to the entrance of the building.

1. Switch to the South Elevation View.

2. Click on the south tower wall.

3. Click on the Edit Profile tool in the Modify|Walls contextual tab, Mode panel.

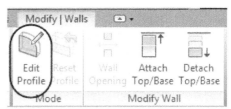

Edit Profile Tool

4. The outline of the wall will turn magenta.

Magenta Outline of Tower Wall

5. Modify the outline as shown.
   - You may include dimensions to help with the size and shape.
   - Add reference planes to aid in creating the arched surface.

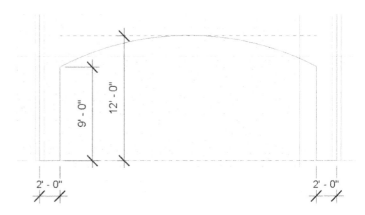

Outline Modified

6. Click the Green Check to create the opening.

7. Repeat the process for the east tower wall.

    - The arc portion will have a different radius due to the shorter wall.

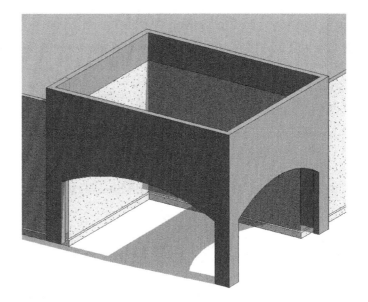

Tower Wall Openings Created

Adding the Roof to the Tower Walls

Next you will add the roof to the Tower. The roof will be higher than the roof for the main building. You will use the same roof type.

1. Go to the T.O. Roof View.

2. Set the Underlay to T.O. WALL. You should see the tower wall edges as grayscale.
    - You may add the roof in any plan view.
    - Check to make sure that the base level is set to T.O Tower and the Base Offset From Level is set to -4'-0".

3. Click on the roof tool and select the Steel Truss - Insulation on Metal Deck – EPDM roof type.

4. When creating the roof footprint, use the Pick Lines option and click the inside face of the line representing the metal

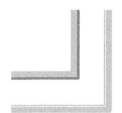

Roof Footprint Edge at Lower Left Corner of Tower

5. Click the Green Check top add the roof. Your roof should look like this...

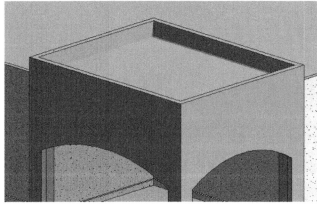

Tower Roof Added

6. This is the end of Part 7 and Tutorial 1. Save your file as CL1-7.

Tutorial 2 - Adding Curtain Walls and Mullions

Part 1	Adding the Curtain Wall
Part 2	Adding the Curtain Grids and Mullions
Part 3	Adding the Mullions and Curtain Wall Door (East Elevation)

Starting the Tutorial

1. Open the drawing file from Tutorial 1 named CL1-7.

2. Save the file as CL2-1.

CL2-1 - Adding the Curtain Wall

1. Switch to the First Floor plan view.

2. Hide the Tower walls and Roof elements.

3. Go to the Architecture Tab, Wall Tool. Select the Curtain Wall 1 wall type. Use the settings below for the properties.

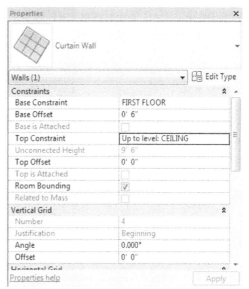

Curtain Wall Settings

4. To locate the ends of the curtain wall, create two reference planes 2'-0" from the centers of each wall.
   (Dimensions are not required.)

Curtain Wall Edges

5. When adding the curtain wall:
   - Pick the center of the concrete wall.
   - Start the wall from the reference plane on the right and drag to the plane on the left.
   - After adding the wall, check that the flip arrows are on the outside.

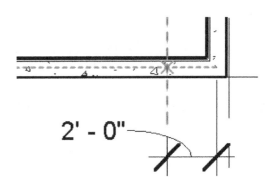

**Snapping on Reference Plane
for Start of Curtain Wall**

6. Once you have added the wall use the Cut Geometry in the Modify Tab, Geometry Panel to remove the overlapping area. Pick the Concrete Wall first and then the Curtain Wall.

7. Your wall should look like this...

Curtain Wall Placed

8. Delete or hide the two reference planes.

9. This is the end of Part 1. Save your file as CL2-1.

CL2-2 - Adding the Curtain Grids and Mullions

1. Continuing from the CL2-1 file, save the file and then save the file as CL2-2.
2. Open the South Elevation view.
3. Hide the Tower walls and Roof elements.
4. Go to the Curtain Grid tool in the Architecture tab, Build panel.
5. To add grid lines:
   - To add vertical grid lines pick on bottom horizontal edge of the Curtain Wall.
   - When adding the vertical lines, create eight lines and then chain dimension. To equally space the lines press the EQ toggle.
   - To add horizontal grid lines, pick on the right or left edge of the Curtain Wall.
   - Use the diagram below for the measurements.
6. After the grids are placed, delete the dimensions. When the warning box appears, click the OK button to leave the grids constrained.

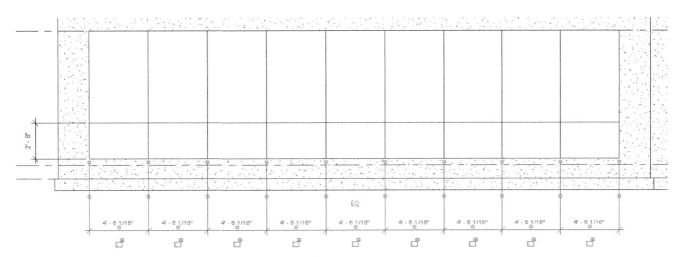

Equally Spaced Grids

7. Go to the Mullion tool in the Architecture tab, Build panel.
8. To place mullions on all of the grids lines at once, select All Grid Lines in the Placement box.
9. Mouse over one of the grid lines. When they all select, click the mouse.
10. The mullions appear. You will need to modify how they intersect.

11. Use the join toggle at the ends of each mullion segment. When the toggle is clicked the join will change.

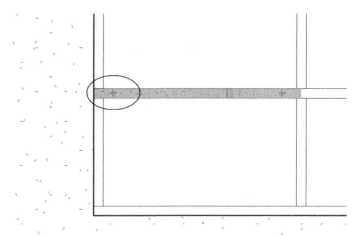

Toggling Mullion Joins

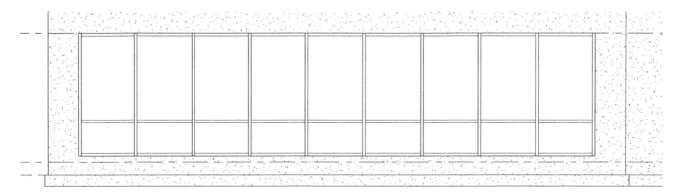

Before Modifying Mullion Joins

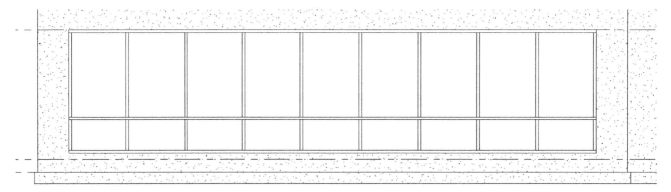

After Modifying Mullion Joins

12. This is the end of Part 2. Save your file as CL2-2.

CL2-3 - Adding the Mullions and Curtain Wall Door (East Elevation)

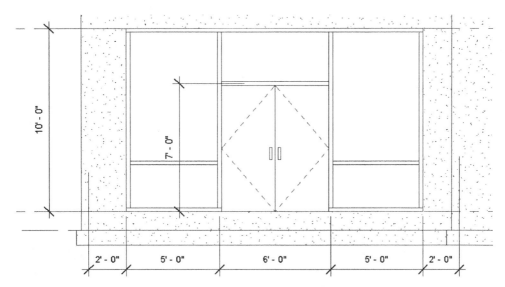

Main Entry Curtain Wall with Door

1. Continuing from the CL2-2 file, save the file and then save the file as CL2-3.

2. Switch to the First Floor view.

3. Create two reference planes from the centers of the two walls.

4. Add a second Curtain Wall. The size of the wall is 10'-0" high and 16'-0" long. The wall is 2'-0" from the edge and is measured from the wall centerline. Use the Cut Geometry Tool as before.

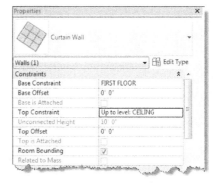

Main Entry Curtain Wall Settings

5. Hide the Tower walls and Roof elements.

6. Switch to the East Elevation View. Locate the grids as shown. (Dimensions are not required.)

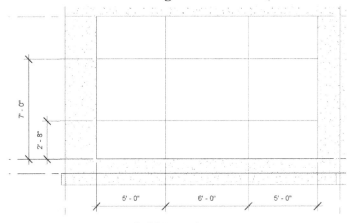

Grid Locations

7. Add the mullions and set up the joins. When adding the mullions use the Grid Line Segment setting in the Placement panel.

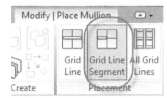

Grid Line Segment Tool

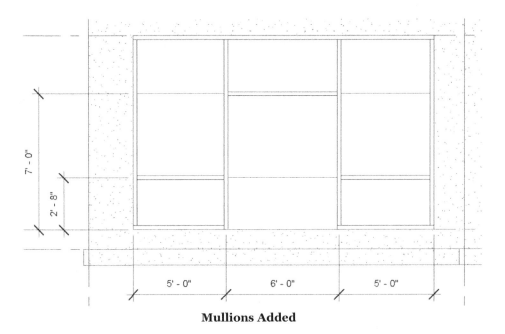

Mullions Added

8. Remove the extra grid segments. Click on the 7'-0" high curtain grin and then the Add/Remove Segments tool in the Curtain Grid Panel.

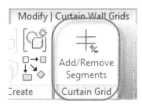

Add/Remove Segments Tool

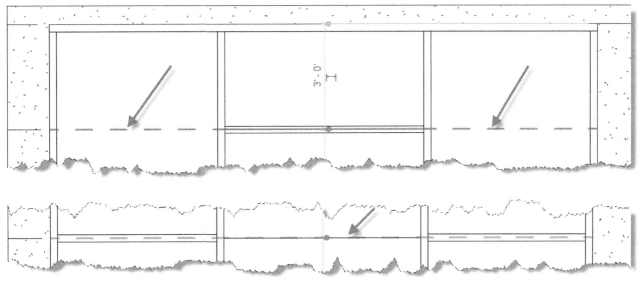

Segments to Remove

9. Next you will add the door to the curtain wall. You will need to load the door type. Since this is a curtain wall, you will need to use the Curtain Wall Dbl Glass door type. This door type is located in the Doors folder under the US Imperial folder.

10. To place the door, you will first need to mouse over the edge of the panel. Then press the tab key until the outline turns blue.

11. Click on the panel without moving the mouse.

12. In the Properties window select the Curtain Wall Dbl Glass door.

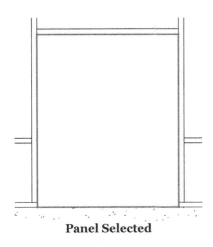

Panel Selected

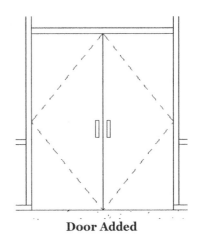

Door Added

13. Switch to the First Floor view, tag the door and dimension the curtain wall.
    (You will need to adjust the dimensions slightly.)

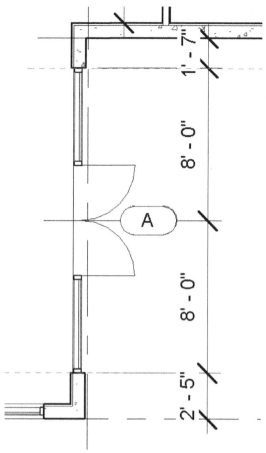

Curtain Wall Dimensioned and Tagged

14. This is the end of Part 3 and Tutorial 2. Save your file as CL2-3.

Tutorial 3 – Creating the Commercial Restrooms	
Part 1	Inserting the Fixtures and Partitions
Part 2	Changing the Floor Surface Material of the Restrooms
Part 3	Creating the Floor Plan Callout and Modifying the Restroom Sinks
Part 4	Creating the Interior Elevation Views of the Restrooms

Starting the Tutorial

1. Open the drawing file from Tutorial 2 named CL2-3.
2. Save the file as CL3-1.

CL3-1 - Inserting the Fixtures and Partitions

Back in Tutorial 1 you laid out the walls for the restrooms. Now you will add the fixtures and partitions.

1. Go to the First Floor Plan view.
2. Refer to the diagram below for the fixtures and partitions you will need. You may have to load the family files for some of these.

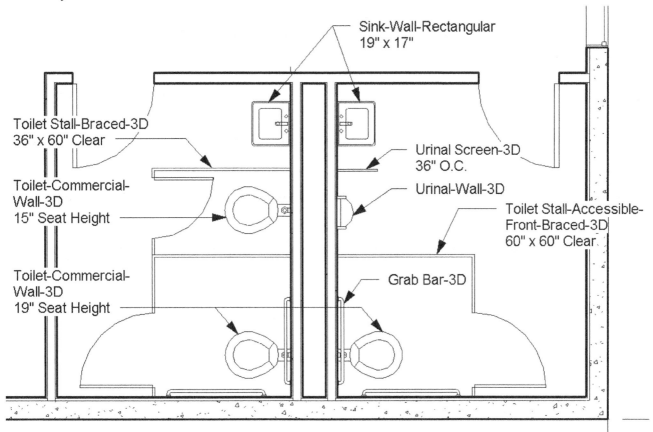

Commercial Restrooms Fixtures and Partitions

3. Refer to the next diagram for placement.

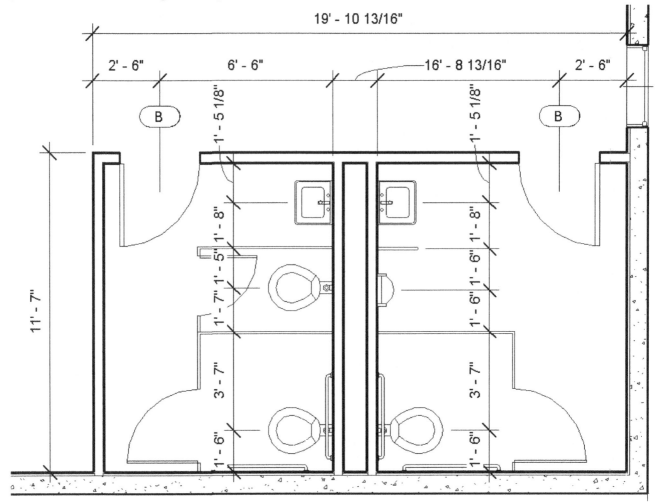

Location of Restroom Fixtures and Partitions

4. This is the end of Part 1. Save your file as CL3-1.

CL3-2 - Changing the Floor Surface Material of the Restrooms

The floor of the restroom is different from the rest of the building. Rather than create a new floor, you will change the surface pattern of the restroom floor.

1. Continuing from the CL3-1 file, save the file and then save the file as CL3-2.

2. Open the First Floor View.

3. Zoom in on the Men's and Women's restrooms.

4. If you can't see the surface pattern of the carpet, turn on the surface pattern toggle in Visibility/Graphic Override.

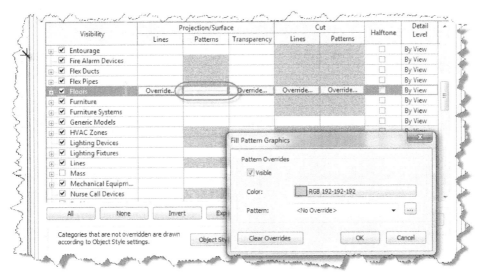

Visibility/Graphic Overrides

5. Click on the Split Face tool. The tool is located in the Modify ribbon, Geometry panel.

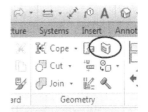

Split Face Tool

6. Mouse over the edge of the floor boundary. When it highlights, click to select. You will know that you have selected it when it gives the description of the floor slab at the bottom left side of the screen.

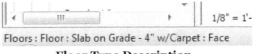

Floor Type Description

7. After you have clicked on the boundary the walls will turn gray and the boundary will turn light orange.

8. In the Draw panel, click on the pick lines tool. Click on the inside edge of the sets of walls that make up the Women's restrooms.

9. As you are clicking on the walls you will need to use the Trim/Extend tool to join the magenta lines together. (If you wish to delete the face, mouse over of the boundary and click to select then press the delete key.)

10. The final version will look like this...

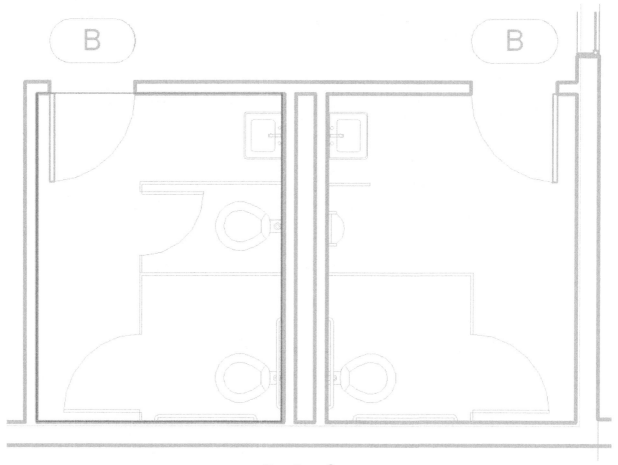

Face Boundary

11. Click the green check when finished.

12. Repeat the process for the other restroom.

13. Once you have completed the two faces you will then paint the surface with a tile pattern. You will need to turn on the surface pattern.

14. Go to the Manage tab, Setting panel and click on the Materials tool.

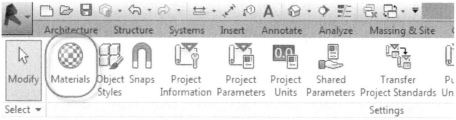

Materials Tool

15. The Material Browser dialog box will open. Search for the Tile material. Select the Tile, Porcelain, 4in material.

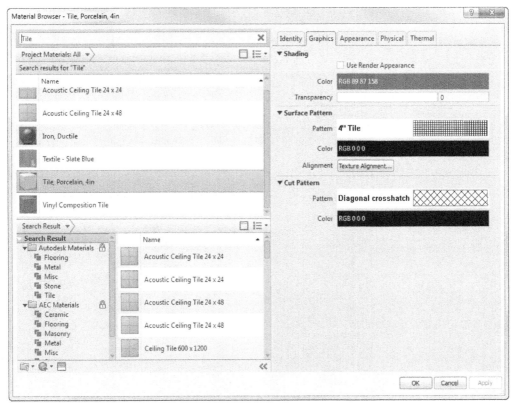

Material Browser Dialog Box

16. After loading, right click on the material and pick Duplicate and then rename the material, Tile, Porcelain, 8in.

17. Edit the material in the area to the right. Select the pattern in the Surface Pattern area and select 8" Tile for the pattern.

18. Click on the Appearance tab at the top right. Click on the arrow next to Relief Pattern and the sample image of the material pattern.

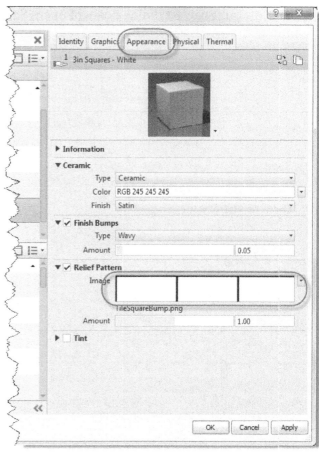

Appearance Tab

19. The Texture Editor box opens. Scroll down and change the Size X and Size Y settings to 1.50. This will change the rendered size of the tiles to 8". Click done and then OK in the Material Browser dialog box.

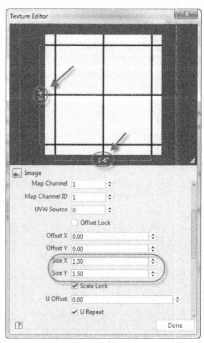

Texture Editor Box

20. Click on the Paint tool in the Modify tab, Geometry panel.

Paint Tool

21. The Material Browser dialog box will open. Type Tile in the search box at the top and then select the Tile, Porcelain, 8in material.

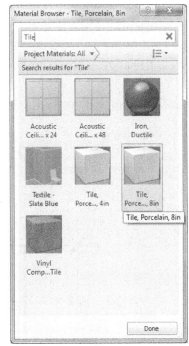

Material Browser

22. With the dialog box still open, click inside each restroom. The pattern will change to the 8" tile pattern. Press the Done button when finished.

23. The restrooms will now look like this...

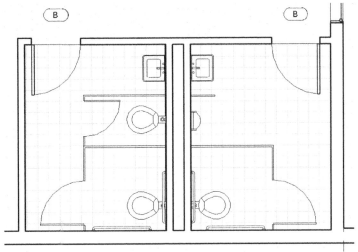

Tile Material Added to Restrooms

24. This is the end of Part 2. Save your file as CL3-2.

CL3-3 - Creating the Floor Plan Callout

Since the restrooms are detailed it would be difficult to show the fixture locations at 1/4"=1'-0" scale. You will create a callout that will allow you to show the restrooms as a separate view.

1. Continuing from the CL3-2 file, save the file and then save the file as CL3-3.

2. Continue in the First Floor view. Zoom in on the two restrooms.

3. Go to the Callout tool. The tool is located in the View tab, Create panel.

4. Click above and to the left of the restrooms then drag down and to the right to enclose the area. A callout boundary will appear as you do this.

5. Click on the edge of the boundary. Handles will appear. Use these to drag the bubble up to the top, left corner.

6. The callout area will look like this...

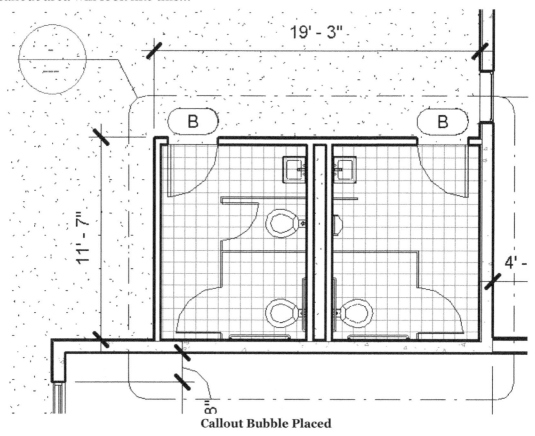

Callout Bubble Placed

7. A new Floor Plan view is created called Callout of First Floor Plan. Later you will drag the view onto a sheet. The bubble will fill in automatically.

8. Open the Callout of FIRST FLOOR view.

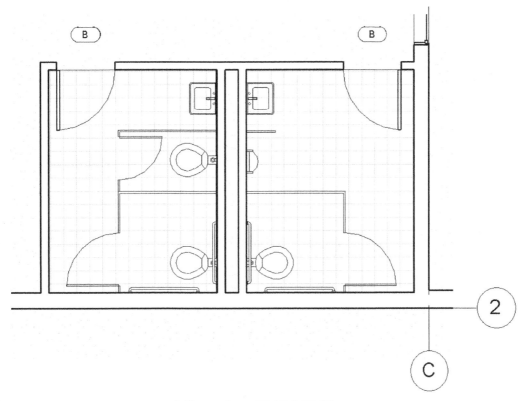

Callout of FIRST FLOOR View

You may notice that the material under the sinks is not masked. You will modify the sinks to mask the material.

9. Right-click on one of the sinks and click on Edit Family. This will open the family file for the sink.

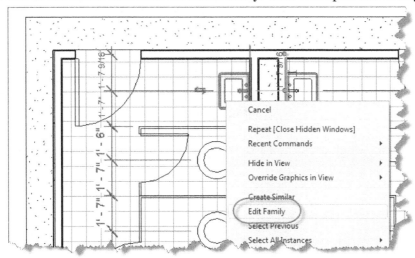

Editing the Sink Family

10. In the family file, open the Floor Line view.

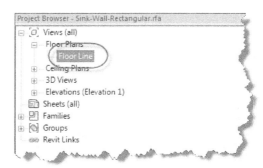

Floor Line View

11. The view opens. Zoom in on the sink.

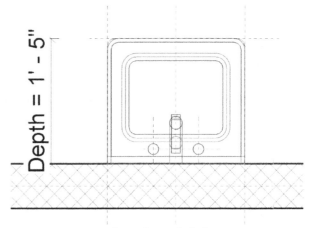

Plan View of Sink

12. Click on the Masking Region tool in the Annotate tab, Detail panel.

Masking Region Tool

13. The view will turn gray. Click on the Pick Lines option in the Draw panel.

Pick Lines Option

14. Click on the lines that make up the outside edges of the sink. The lines will appear as thin and dark. (Not magenta.)

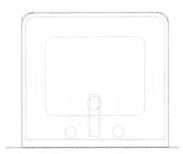

Masking Region Boundary Picked

15. Click the Green Check. If you get an error message you will need to continue with the sketch and trim the corners.

16. Click on the Load into Project tool. When the Family Already Exists alert box opens, click on the Overwrite the existing version option.

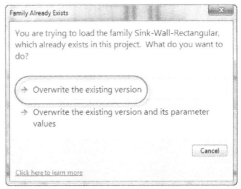

Family Already Exists Alert Box

17. The material beneath the two sinks is now masked.

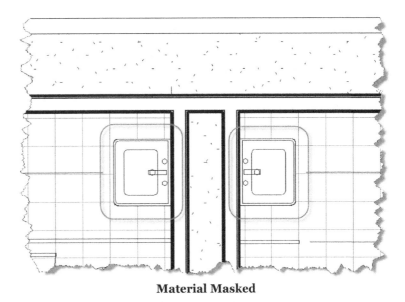

Material Masked

18. This is the end of Part 3. Save your file as CL3-3.

CL3-4 - Creating the Interior Elevation Views of the Restrooms

1. Continuing from the CL3-3 file, save the file and then save the file as CL3-4.

2. Open the Callout of First Floor Plan view.

3. Go to the View tab, Create panel, Elevation tool. Left-click on the tool. In the type selector make sure the Interior Elevation type is selected.

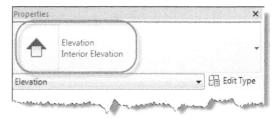

Interior Elevation Type Selected

4. Click inside the Women's Restroom and drag towards the right wall until the arrow is pointing to the right.

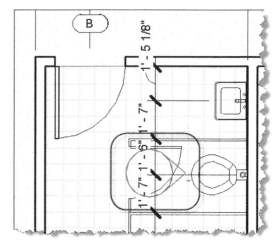

Placing Elevation Marker

5. Click to place the marker. A new view is created called Elevation 1-a. Rename the view Women's Restroom.

6. You will need to adjust the crop window of the view to match the example.

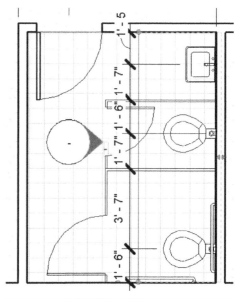

Crop Window - Plan View

7. Repeat the process for the Men's Restroom. Name the view accordingly.

8. The scale of both Interior Elevation views is 1/4"=1'-0".

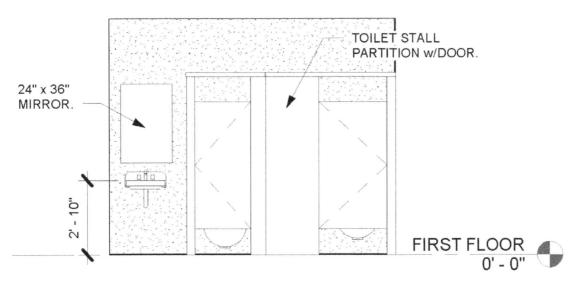

Women's Room Elevation

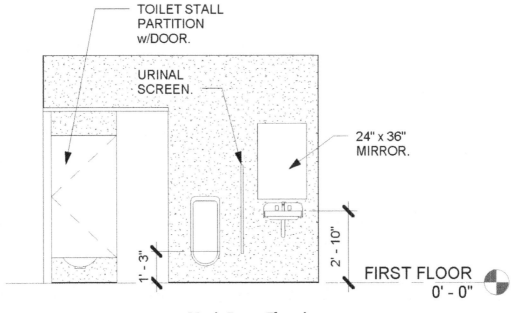

Men's Room Elevation

9. This is the end of Part 4 and Tutorial 3. Save your file as CL3-4.

Tutorial 4 – Creating the Schedules and Room Legend	
Part 1	Creating the Door Schedule
Part 2	Creating the Window Schedule
Part 3	Adding the Room Tags
Part 4	Creating the Room Finish Schedule
Part 5	Creating the Room Legend

Starting the Tutorial

1. Open the drawing file from Tutorial 3 named CL3-4.

2. Save the file as CL4-1.

CL4-1 - Creating the Door Schedule

1. In the Project Browser double click on the Door Schedule view under the Schedules/Quantities category.

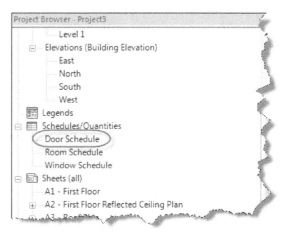

Door Schedule in Project Browser

2. The Door Schedule view will open. Some of the fields will already be filled out.

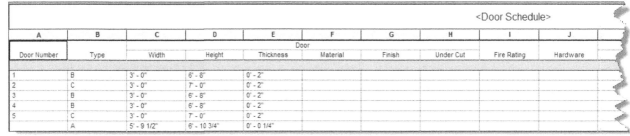

A	B	C	D	E	F	G	H	I	J
				Door					
Door Number	Type	Width	Height	Thickness	Material	Finish	Under Cut	Fire Rating	Hardware
1	B	3' - 0"	6' - 8"	0' - 2"					
2	C	3' - 0"	7' - 0"	0' - 2"					
3	B	3' - 0"	6' - 8"	0' - 2"					
4	B	3' - 0"	6' - 8"	0' - 2"					
5	C	3' - 0"	7' - 0"	0' - 2"					
	A	5' - 9 1/2"	6' - 10 3/4"	0' - 0 1/4"					

\<Door Schedule\>

Default Door Schedule

3. Instead of modifying this Door Schedule, you will delete the existing schedule and create a new one. Right-click on the Door Schedule view and select Delete.

4. Click on the Schedules/Quantities tool in the View tab, Create panel.

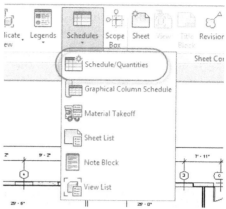

Schedule/Quantities Tool

5. In the New Schedule dialog box select Doors in the Category window.

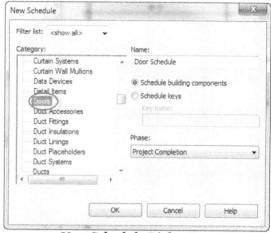

New Schedule Dialog Box

6. In the New Schedule dialog box add the Type Mark, Width, Height, Thickness, and Type fields.

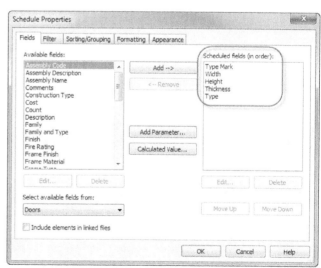

Schedule Properties Dialog Box

7. Click on the Sorting/Grouping tab and select Type Mark as the Sort by: setting. Uncheck the Itemize every instance checkbox at the bottom left side of the dialog box.

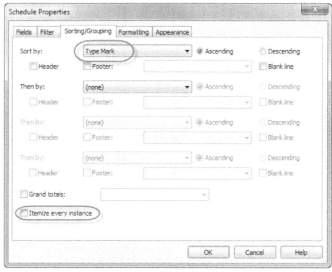

Sort by: Type Mark

8. Click on the Formatting tab and set the Type Mark, Width, Height, and Thickness fields to Center alignment.

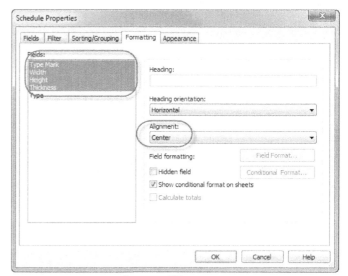

Center Alignment

9. Click on the Appearance tab and uncheck the Blank row before data checkbox. Check the Outline: checkbox and set the lines to Wide Lines.

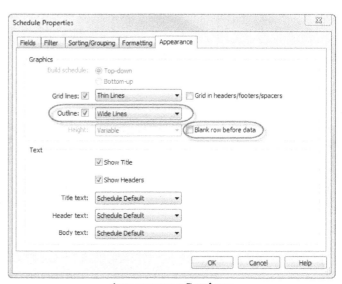

Appearance Settings

10. Select the header text and click on the Font tool in the appearance tab. Set the Header Text to 9/64" and check the Bold checkbox. Set the Door Schedule text to 1/4" and Bold.

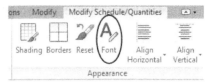

Font Tool

- You will also change the text in the header boxes to all caps and match the words in the example below.

Edit Font Dialog Box

11. Click on the Format Unit tool in the Parameters panel. Set the parameters settings as shown.

Format Units Settings

12. Change the thickness of the Curtain Wall Dbl Glass door to 1/4". All the other fields are based on the door properties and will be correct.

13. Stretch the TYPE field so that the entire field is visible.

14. The Door Schedule will now look like this...

\<DOOR SCHEDULE\>				
A	B	C	D	E
MARK	WIDTH	HEIGHT	THICK.	TYPE
A	5' - 9 1/2"	6' - 10 3/4"	1/4"	Curtain Wall Dbl Glass
B	3' - 0"	6' - 8"	2"	36" x 80"
C	3' - 0"	7' - 0"	2"	36" x 84"

Door Schedule View

15. This is the end of Part 1. Save your file as CL4-1.

CL4-2 - Creating the Window Schedule

1. Continuing from the CL4-1 file, save the file and then save the file as CL4-2.
2. Delete the existing Window Schedule.
3. In the New Schedule dialog box add the Type Mark, Width, Height, and Type fields.
4. Sort by Type Mark.
5. Align all the fields by Center.
6. Remove the Blank row.
7. Set the Appearance the same as the Door Schedule.
8. Modify the title and header text.
9. The Window Schedule should now look like this...

A	B	C	D
<WINDOW SCHEDULE>			
MARK	WIDTH	HEIGHT	TYPE
1	3' - 0"	4' - 0"	36" x 48"
2	3' - 0"	6' - 0"	36" x 72"
3	4' - 0"	6' - 0"	48" x 72"
4	4' - 0"	3' - 0"	48" x 36"

Window Schedule View

10. This is the end of Part 2. Save your file as CL4-2.

CL4-3 - Adding the Room Tags

1. Continuing from the CL4-2 file, save the file and then save the file again as CL4-3.

2. Unhide the tower walls. (Do this in all plan views.)

3. Refer the diagram below for reference. The dimensions and schedule symbols have been hidden for clarity.
   (Your square footage may be slightly different.)

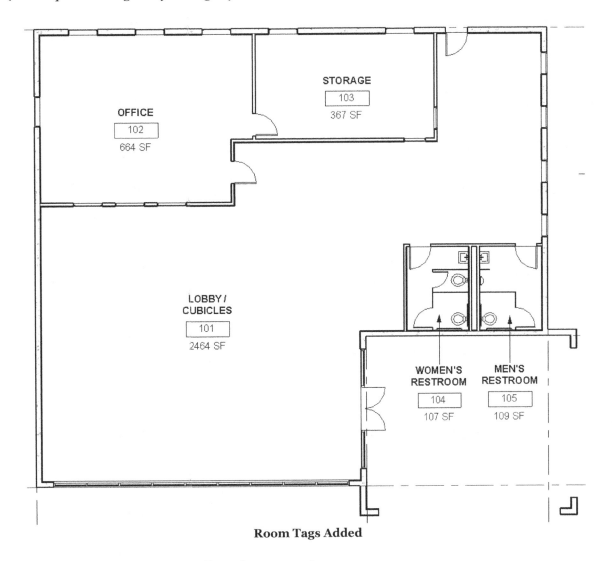

Room Tags Added

Before you can add the tags you will need to create the rooms.

4. Click on the Room tool in the Architecture ribbon, Room & Area panel. If you select the Tag on Placement toggle, the tags will be placed at the same time.

5. Use the Room Tag With Area tag.

6. When adding the tags for the restrooms, you will need to check the leader box in the options bar. Also, click on the Edit Type button below the Type Selector then change the Leader Arrowhead to Arrow Filled 30 Degree.

7. After the tags have been added, edit the room labels as shown in the example above.

8. This is the end of Part 3. Save your file as CL4-3.

CL4-4 - Creating the Room Finish Schedule

1. Continuing from the CL4-3 file, save the file and then save the file again as CL4-4.

2. Delete the existing Room Finish schedule.

3. In the New Schedule dialog box, select the Room category.

4. Select the Number, Name, Floor Finish, Ceiling Finish, Wall Finish, and Area fields.

5. Set up the schedule the same way as the Door and Window Schedules.
   - If you cannot see the rooms you may need to change the Phase from Project completion to New Construction. (This is done in the Properties Palette.)

Phasing Set to New Construction

Schedule Fields Added

6. Add the Grand Total line at the bottom. Do this by checking the Grand totals: checkbox at the bottom of the Sorting/Grouping tab.

7. Select the Title and totals pull-down.

Sorting/Grouping Settings

8. Some of the fields will be blank. You will need to fill-in the Floor Finish, Ceiling Finish, and Wall Finish fields. This will also fill in the Properties box for each room.

9. The schedule will look like this when finished...

\<ROOM FINISH SCHEDULE\>					
A	B	C	D	E	F
NUMBER	ROOM NAME	FLOOR	CEILING	WALL	AREA
101	LOBBY / CUBICLES	CARPET	2'X4' ACT	GYP BD	2395 SF
102	OFFICE	CARPET	2'X2' ACT	GYP BD	620 SF
103	STORAGE	CONCRETE	GYP BD	GYP BD	345 SF
104	WOMEN'S RESTROOM	TILE	GYP BD	GYP BD	96 SF
105	MEN'S RESTROOM	TILE	GYP BD	GYP BD	103 SF
Grand total					3560 SF

Room Finish Schedule View

10. This is the end of Part 4. Save your file as CL4-4.

CL4-5 - Creating the Room Legend

The last item in this Tutorial is to create a room legend. The room legend is used to color code the various rooms in a structure and to provide a key or legend with the drawing. The process with involve creating a duplicate of the floor plan view and modifying it.

1. Continuing from the CL4-4 file, save the file and then save the file again as CL4-5.

2. Go to the First Floor Plan view.

3. Right-click on the name of the view in the Project Browser.

4. Select Duplicate View and then Duplicate with Detailing.

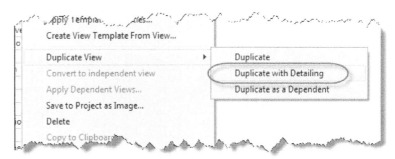

Duplicate with Detailing Option

5. A new view called Copy of FIRST FLOOR appears in the browser.

6. Right-click on the new view and rename it FIRST FLOOR PLAN – COLOR LEGEND.

7. Hide the following items: Dimensions, Door Tags, Window Tags, Grids, and Elevation Markers.

8. At this point your drawing will look like this...

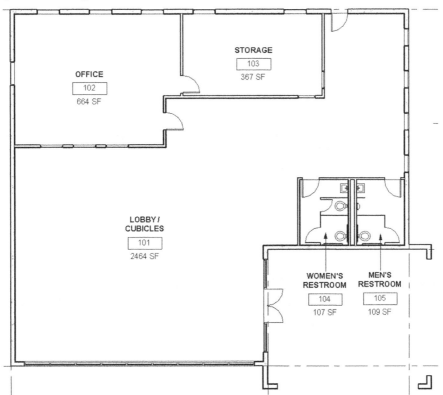

FIRST FLOOR PLAN - COLOR LEGEND View

9. Go to the Annotate tab, Color Fill panel and select the Color Fill Legend tool.

Color Fill Legend Tool

10. Attached to the cursor will be a box with the words No color scheme assigned to view.

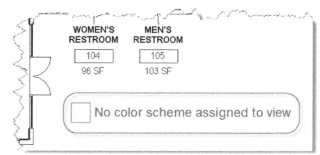

No Color Scheme Assigned to View

11. This is the legend. Place it at the bottom right corner of the view.

12. The Choose Space Type and Color Scheme dialog box opens. Change the Space Type: setting to Rooms and the Color Scheme: setting to Name.

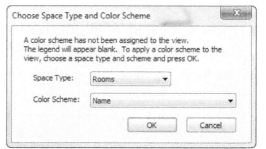

Choose Space Type and Color Scheme Dialog Box

13. Press the OK button.

14. The rooms will now have colors assigned to them.

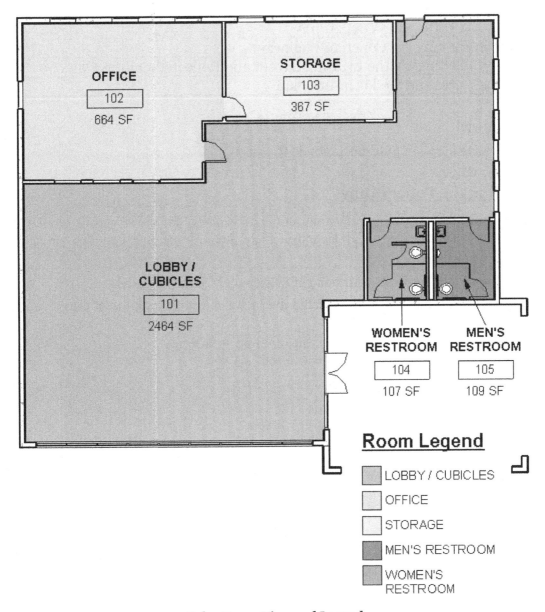

Color Room View and Legend

15. This is the end of Part 5 and Tutorial 4. Save your file as CL4-5.

Tutorial 5 – Creating the Site Elements and Reflected Ceiling Plan

Part 1	Creating the Topography
Part 2	Adding the Concrete Walkway
Part 3	Setting Up the Lighting Layout and Reflected Ceiling Plan
Part 4	Creating the Furniture Plan

Starting the Tutorial

1. Open the drawing file from Tutorial 4 named CL4-5.

2. Save the file as CL5-1.

CL5-1 - Creating the Topography

In this tutorial you will create topography and a concrete walkway for the structure. Unlike an actual site, the topography will be perfectly flat. Usually a slight incline/decline is included for water runoff.

1. Open the Site Plan view.

2. Go to the Toposurface Tool in the Massing and Site tab, Model Site panel. ...

3. The Place Point tool is automatically selected. Before placing your points, set the elevation to -0'-6".

4. Place four points around the perimeter of the building as shown.
   (They do not need to be in the exact same location.)

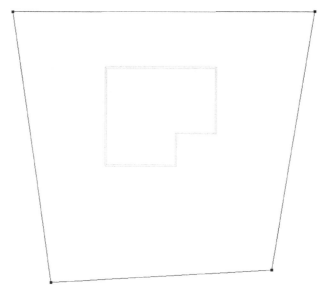

Perimeter of Topography

5. Click the green check to complete the process.

6. Click on the edge of the topography.
   - In the Properties dialog box, change the material to Site – Asphalt.
   - If you do not have this material, create it using the Asphalt, Pavement material located in the Autodesk Materials folder.
   - (You could have also done this while adding the topography).

7. This is the end of Part 1. Save your file as CL5-1.

CL5-2 - Creating the Concrete Walkway and Roof Symbols

1. Continuing from the CL5-1 file, save the file and then save the file as CL5-2.

Next you will create a concrete walkway for the building. This is separate from the concrete floor of the building and will be placed around the outside edge of the structure.

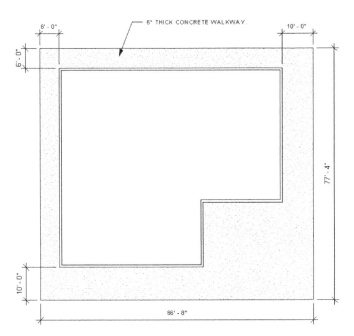

Concrete Walkway Dimensions (Tower Walls Hidden)

2. Open the Site Plan View.
3. Go to the Floor tool.

4. Create a 6" thick concrete floor using the dimensions shown above. You will also create an opening that matches the exterior shape of the building. You may use dimensions to help place the magenta lines in the correct locations.

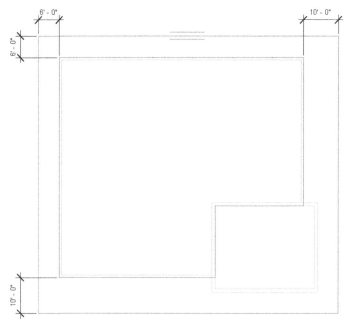

Sketch Boundary for Walkway

5. Create a floor slab type called Exterior Sidewalk – Slab on grade 6". Set the slab properties to 6" thick concrete. Set the surface pattern to Sand. The Level will be set to First Floor.

6. Click the green check. The layout dimensions will turn off.

7. Unhide the Tower walls and Roof if necessary.

8. Add the note for the walkway.

9. Switch to the Roof Plan view.

10. To add the symbols for the roof, use the Detail Line tool in the Annotate tab, Detail panel.

11. Place the lines and circles as shown. Use 8" radius for the 14 circles.

12. Place the notes as shown.

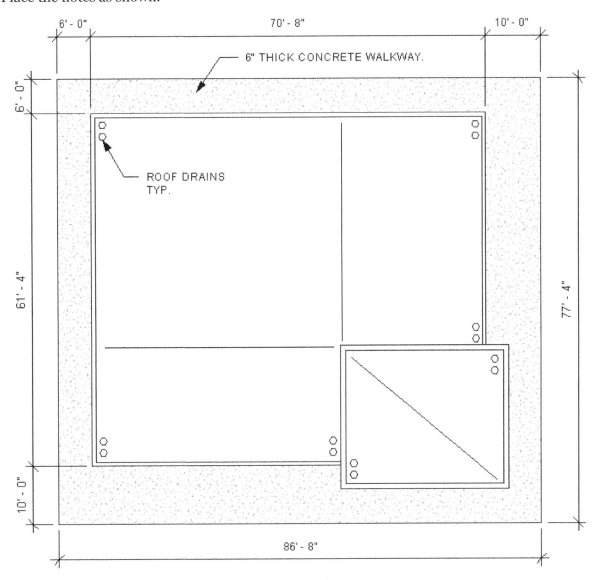

Roof Notes and Dimensions

13. This is the end of Part 2. Save your file as CL5-2.

CL5-3 - Creating the Reflected Ceiling Plan

1. Continuing from the CL5-2 file, save the file and then save the file again as CL5-3.

2. Hide the Tower walls and Roof elements.

3. Open the First Floor Ceiling Plan view.

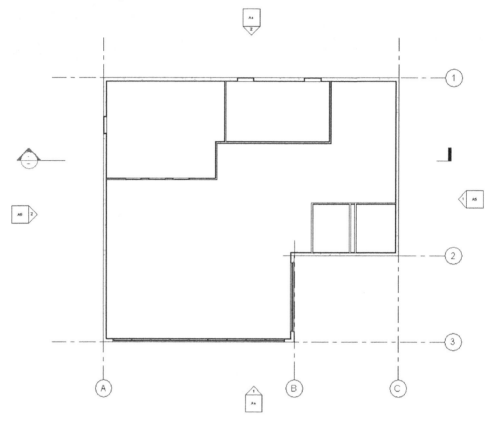

First Floor Reflected Ceiling Plan View

4. Click on the Ceiling Tool located in the Architecture ribbon, Build panel.

Ceiling Tool

5. Select the Compound Ceiling 2' x 4' ACT Ceiling.

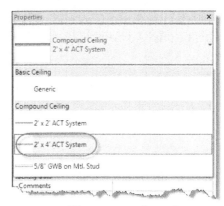

Ceiling Type Selected

6. Click inside the Lobby/Cubicle area. The boundary will highlight in red and the ceiling panels will appear after clicking.

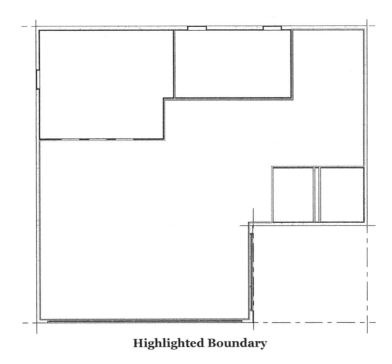

Highlighted Boundary

7. Select the Troffer Light – Lens 2'x4'(4 Lamp) -227V.

8. Place the lamps as shown on the example. Align the edges of the lamps with the ceiling tiles.

9. Place the five diffusers as shown. Use the Square Supply Diffuser - Mask 24" x 24" component. (This family is available in the custom family folder on the website.)

10. Place the two returns as shown. Use the Square Return Register 24" x 24" - Mask component. (This family is available in the custom family folder on the website.)

Lobby/Cubicle Lights, Diffusers, and Registers Placed

11. Start a new ceiling. Select the Compound Ceiling 2' x 2' ACT Ceiling.

12. Click inside the Office Area.

13. Place the lights, diffusers, and return as shown. Use the Troffer Light – Lens 2'x2' (4 Lamp) -120V component for the lights. Use the same diffuser and return as before.

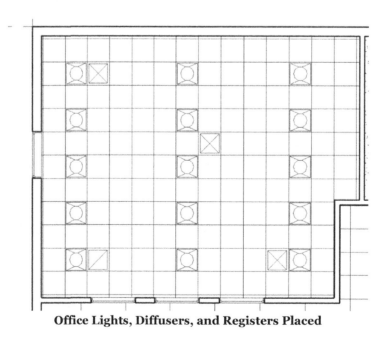

Office Lights, Diffusers, and Registers Placed

14. Start a new ceiling. Select the GWB on Mtl. Stud ceiling type.

15. Click inside the Storage Area.

16. Place the lights and diffusers as shown. Use the Downlight – Recessed Can 8" Incandescent – 277V for the lights. Equally space the lights as shown. Use the equality constraint as shown. Use the same diffuser and return as before. Hide the dimensions after locating the lights.

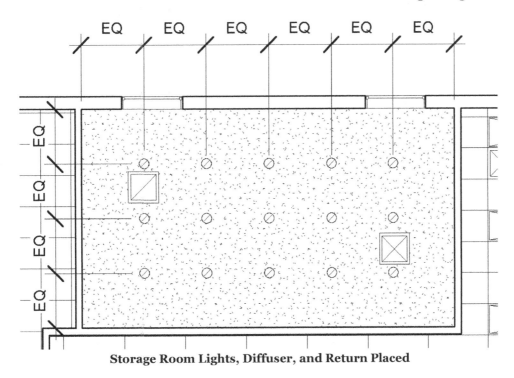

Storage Room Lights, Diffuser, and Return Placed

17. Zoom in on the Restroom area.

18. Select the Ceiling tool. Using the same ceiling type as the Storage Area, click inside the Women's Restroom Area.

19. Place the lights and diffusers as shown.
    - Use the Downlight – Recessed Can 8" Incandescent – 277V for the lights.
    - Space the lights approximately 3'-9" from each other and center on the ceiling.
    - Use the Square Supply Diffuser - Mask 12"x12" for the diffuser and the Square Return Register - Mask 12" x 12" for the return.
    - The Return and Diffuser families are in the custom folder on the website.

20. Repeat the process for the Men's Restroom.

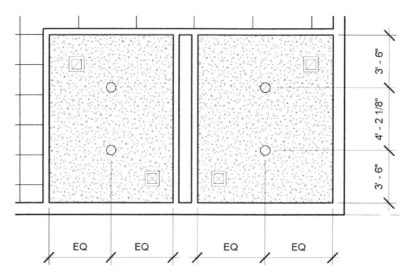

Restroom Lights with Dimensions

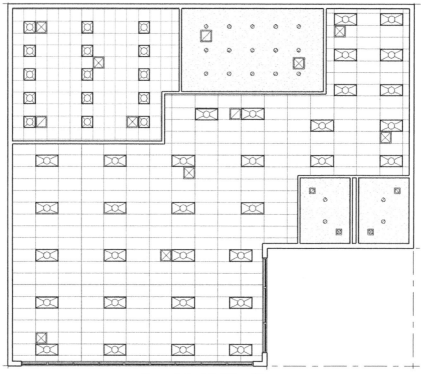

Completed Ceiling Plan

21. This is the end of Part 3. Save your file as CL5-3.

CL5-4 - Creating the Furniture Plan

1. Continuing from the CL5-3 file, save the file and then save the file again as CL5-4.

2. Open the First Floor view.

3. Right click on the view name in the project browser and click Duplicate View, Duplicate.

4. Set the view scale for the view to 3/32" = 1'-0".

5. Click on the Tag All tool in the Annotate tab, Tag Panel.

6. In the Tag All Not Tagged dialog box, select the Room Tags Category and use the Room Tag to tag the rooms.

Tag All Not Tagged Dialog Box

7. The rooms are now tagged. Adjust the location of the tags as shown. You will need to turn on the leaders and arrowheads for the Room Tag family.

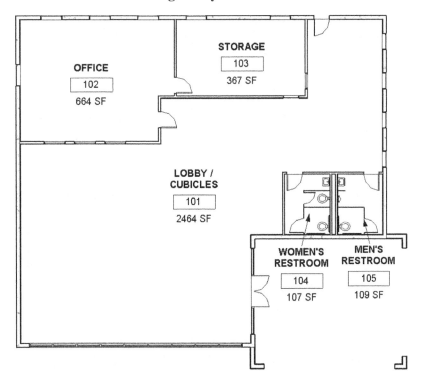

Furniture Plan View with Room Labels

8. Use the chart to select the appropriate furniture:

Room	Furniture	Location
Office	Three – Storage Pedestal (20" x 36" x 36")	Furniture Systems Folder
	One – Desk (72" x 36")	Furniture, Tables Folder
	One – Chair-Executive	Furniture, Seating Folder
	One – Work Station Cubicle (96" x 96")	Furniture Systems Folder
Lobby/ Cubicles	Five – Work Station Cubicle (96" x 96")	Furniture Systems Folder
Storage	None	
Restrooms	No Furniture, only Fixtures	

Notes:
- This is the minimum amount of furniture.
- You may additional chairs and office equipment if you wish.
- Insert the furniture in the correct location based on the drawing shown.
- Add the notes for the cabinets and cubicles.

9. When finished, your furniture plan should look like this...

Furniture Added

10. This is the end of Part 4 and Tutorial 5. Save your file as CL5-4.

Tutorial 6 – Adding the Roof Cap and Setting Up the Design Options	
Part 1	Adding the Roof Cap and Changing the Wall Material
Part 2	Creating the Tower Wall Design Options
Part 3	Creating the Tower Roof Design Options
Part 4	Creating and Annotating the Wall Sections and Details
Part 5	Setting Up the Design Option Views

Note: All screenshots are from the Autodesk® Revit® software.

Starting the Tutorial

1. Open the last file from Tutorial Five, CL5-4.

2. Save the file as CL6-1.

In this tutorial you will add the roof cap to the main building and tower walls. You will also set up two different design options of the project. One will show two different roof styles for the tower and the other will show two entry openings for the tower walls. You will then setup four different of views that show the different design options.

CL6-1 - Adding the Roof Cap and Changing the Wall Material

To finish up the look of the building you will add coping (parapet cover) cap around the top edge of the exterior and tower walls. You will also change the appearance of the tower wall material.

1. Open the 3D view of the project.

2. Zoom in on the top of the tower portion of the project.

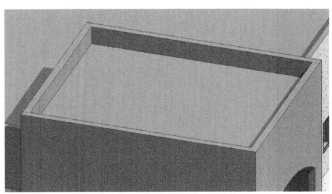

Top Portion of Tower

3. Click on the Component - Model-In-Place tool in the Architecture ribbon, Build panel.

4. In the Family Category and Parameters dialog, choose Roofs for the Family Category. Name the category Coping 1.

5. Click on the Set tool in the Work Plane panel.

Set Tool

6. Click the Pick a plane button.

Pick a plane Button

7. Hover over one of the top surfaces for the tower walls and click.
   - To verify the choice click on the Show toggle in the Work Plane panel. The plane will highlight.

Top Surface of Tower Wall

8. Click the Sweep tool in the Create ribbon, Forms panel.

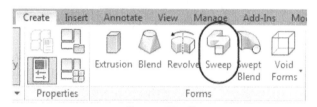

Sweep Tool

9. The view will turn gray. Use the Sketch Path or Pick Path tools to pick the outside corner of the tower walls.

Sketch Path and Pick Path Tools

10. The path will appear as a magenta line.
    - When placing the lines, lock the line to the edge of the tower walls.
    - Click the Green Check when finished.

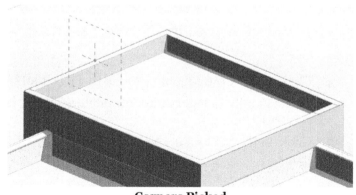

Corners Picked

11. Select the profile called: Sill-Precast : 12" Wide from the profile pulldown. This profile file is preloaded in the template file.

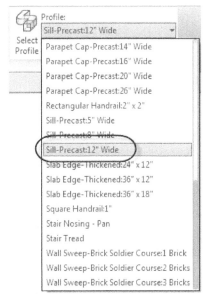

Profile Selected

12. Click the Green Check to add the coping.

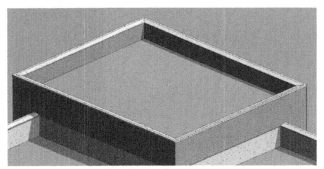

Coping Added

13. If the coping is facing the wrong direction:
   - Double-click on the coping.
   - The coping will turn gray.
   - Look for the profile shape and select it.
   - Click the Flip button to flip the direction of the coping.
   - You may also choose to move the profile back from the edge of the wall a few inches. This is adjusted by changing the dimension for the handle point.
   - When finished with these changes, click the Green Check twice to apply and finish the model.

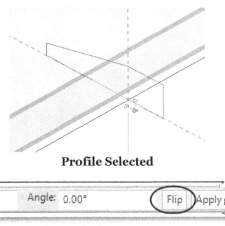

Profile Selected

Flip Button

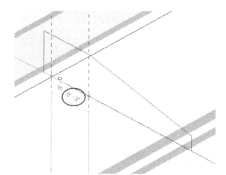

Profile Flipped and Moved 3" Inward

14. Repeat the process for the exterior walls.

   - Change the reference plane to the top of the exterior wall.
   - The sketch path does not need to be a closed loop.

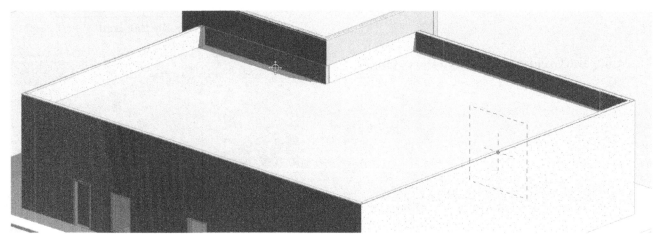

Sketch Path for Exterior Walls

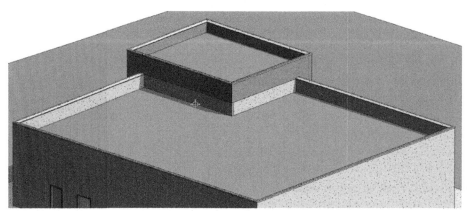

Coping Placed

Next you will update the material of the tower walls. These walls were set to a stucco material back in Tutorial 1. Now you will change the color of the material.

15. Open the Material Browser dialog box.

16. Search for the Stucco material.

17. In the dialog click on the Appearance tab.

18. Click the arrow next to Tint and match the Tint Color as shown.

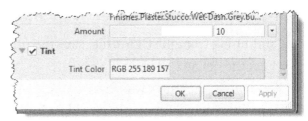

Tint Color Setting

19. Click on the Graphics Tab and check the Use Render Appearance checkbox.

    This will change the material of the wall when the view is shaded.

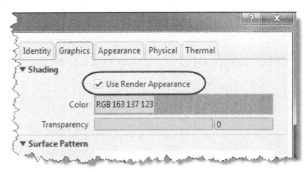

Use Render Appearance Checkbox

20. Click the OK button to close the dialog box and apply the changes.

21. This is the end of Part 1. Save your file as CL6-1.

CL6-2 - Creating the Tower Wall and Tower Roof Design Option Sets

1. Continuing from the CL6-1 file, save the file as CL6-2.

2. Open the default 3D view.

3. Zoom in on the tower walls.

At this point you will set up place holders for the two option sets.

4. Open the Design Options dialog box by clicking on the tool at the bottom of the screen.

Design Options Tool

5. The Design Options dialog box opens.

Design Options Dialog Box

6. Click on the New button under the Option Set.

7. Create two option sets, Tower Wall and Tower Roof

8. With the Tower Wall option set selected, click the New button under the Option area.

9. Create two options, 1 – Arched Opening and 2 – Rectangular Opening.

10. Select the Tower Roof option; click the New button under the Option area.

11. Create two options, 1 – Flat Roof and 2 – Hip Roof.

12. When finished your Design options dialog
box should look like this...

Design Options Added

13. Select the following:
    - The two front tower walls,
    - The two short side walls,
    - The two back walls that are above the exterior walls of the building.
    - When you are finished selecting the elements, you will have six elements selected. Check for this at the bottom right of the screen next to the filter symbol.

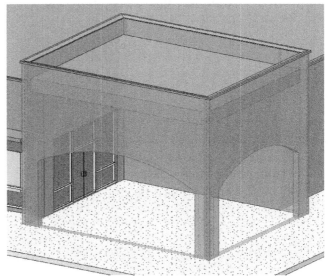

Elements Selected

14. Click the Add to Set tool at the bottom of the screen next to the Design Options tool.

Add to Set Tool

15. The Add to Design Option Set dialog box opens. Select the Tower Wall option if necessary. Click the OK to close the box and add the elements to the two options.

    Note:
    What just happened is the six elements that were selected were removed from the Main Model. Then these two sets of the elements were added back into the model, one for each of the Design options. This way you will be able to change the second set of elements without affecting the first set.

Add to Design Option Set Dialog Box

16. You will get a warning box that states that the elements highlighted in orange are joined but do not intersect.

    Click the Unjoin Elements button to unjoin the walls and clear the box.

Warning Box

You may notice that you will not be able to select any of the elements. To access these elements you will need to activate one of the design options for the Tower Wall.

17. Click on the Active Design drop-down at the bottom of the screen. Select the first option on the Tower Wall option.

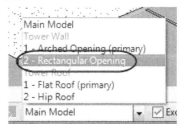

Active Design Option Drop-Down

18. The rest of the model will gray out and you
    will be able to pick the six elements.

    Note:
    Since the Primary Option (#1) will not
    change, you will not be modifying those
    elements.

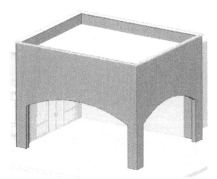

Tower Wall – Option #2 Elements

Now you will modify the opening for the south and east tower walls.

19. Click on the south tower wall.

20. Click the Edit Profile tool.

21. Draw a new profile line starting at the top
    midpoint of the arc.

New Profile Line

22. Delete the arc and trim/extend the horizontal
    line to the two inside vertical lines.

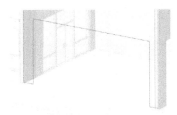

Profile of Rectangular Opening Created

23. Click the Green Check to complete the modification.

24. Repeat the process for the east tower wall.

25. Your model should look like this when finished...

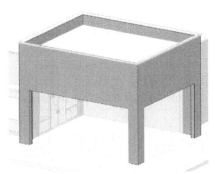

**Completed Tower Wall –
Option #2 – Rectangular Opening**

26. Change the Design Option to Main Model. The Option #2 elements will turn off. Later you will set up a 3D view that will show this option.

27. You may notice a gap between the two tower wall ends.
    This is caused when the tower walls were removed from the Main Model and copied into the Tower Wall design options.

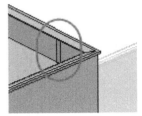

Wall Gap Between Tower Walls

   - If this happens, re-enter the Tower Wall Design Option.
   - Go to the T.O. TOWER view. Zoom in on the corner and drag the wall end to join with the other wall end.
   - If you still see a line at the join, go to the Join tool in the Modify ribbon, Geometry panel.
   - Click on both walls to join them. The line should disappear.
   - You may need to do this for both Tower Wall Design Options.

28. This is the end of Part 2. Save your file as CL6-2.

CL6-3 - Creating the Tower Roof Design Options

You have already created the Design Option for the Tower Roof. Now you will add elements to create a Hip roof structure for the second option.

1. Continuing from the CL6-2 file, save the file as CL6-3.

2. Open the 3d View.

3. Confirm that you are in the Main Model.

4. Select the Flat Roof and the Roof Cap.

5. Cut the elements to the clipboard.

6. Switch to the Tower Roof Option 1 – Flat Roof.

7. Paste the two elements. Use the Aligned to Same Place option.

Aligned to Same Place Option

8. The elements are added to the design option.

   The reason for this is so these elements will not appear in the second roof design option.

   This is all you will need to do for the first roof design option.

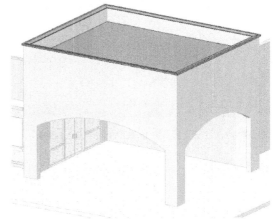

Elements Added to the Design Option

9. Switch to the Tower Roof Option 2 – Hip Roof.

10. There are no elements in this design option. Also, the flat roof and the roof cap are now gone.

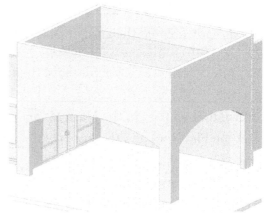

Tower Roof Option 2

11. Open the T.O. Tower view.
12. Click on the Roof by Footprint tool.
    - You will use the Basic Roof Generic – 12" roof style.
    - Use a 2'-0" overhang.
    - Set the roof slope to 4:12.
    - Click the Green check to complete the roof.

Roof Footprint Sketch

13. Return to the 3D View to view the roof.

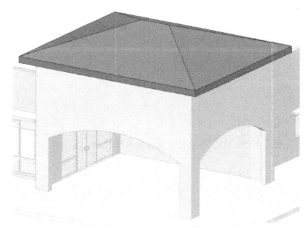

Roof Added to Tower Roof – Option #2

14. This completes second Tower Roof design option.
15. Return to the Main Model.
16. This is the end of Part 3. Save your file as CL6-3.

CL6-4 - Creating and Annotating the Wall Sections and Details

In this part you will create and annotate two wall sections and two details. Wall sections and details are used to show the materials and methods of construction for portions of the structure such as the connections between the floor slab and the exterior wall.

1. Continuing from the CL6-3 file, save the file and then save the file again as CL6-4.

2. Open the Longitudinal Section View.

3. Zoom in on the right side of the building.

4. Click on the Callout tool in the View ribbon, Create panel.

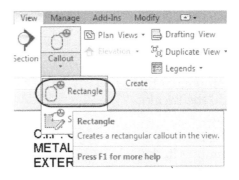

Callout Tool, Rectangle Option

5. Draw a rectangular callout area surrounding the wall, roof, and footer.
   - Move the bubble to the top right or left, away from the text.
   - As you add the section, make sure that the section type is set to Wall Section in the Properties Palette.

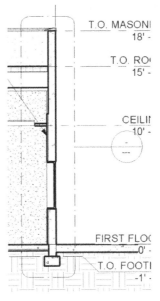

Callout Area

6. Open the Wall Section view. Name the section view: EAST WALL SECTION

7. Add the annotations as shown in the example.
   - If you are not seeing the annotations, click on the crop window and move the edge of the annotation crop (dashed line) away from the view.

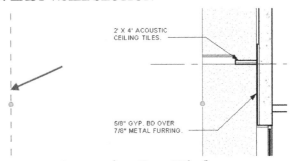

Annotation Crop Window

8. When adding the notes and dimensions:
   - Set the scale of the view to 3/8"=1'-0".
   - Draw the Cant Strip use the Detail Line tool set to Medium Lines.
   - Use the Detail Component tool in Annotate ribbon, Detail panel, Component tool to add the Break Line.
   - The Break Line family is in the custom families folder on the website.
   - When adding the Detail Callout around the Footer, set the callout type to Detail View.
   - The Detail Bubble will fill in with the sheet number after the Wall Section view has been placed on the sheet.
   - Line up the notes vertically when placing the text.

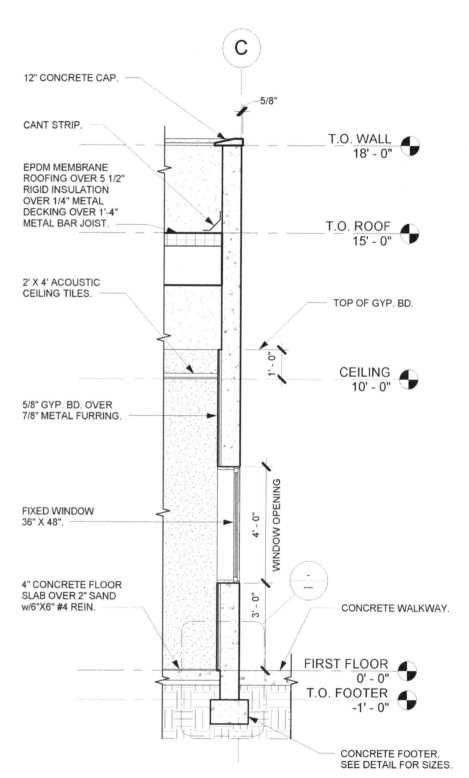

12" CONCRETE CAP.

5/8"

CANT STRIP.

T.O. WALL
18' - 0"

EPDM MEMBRANE ROOFING OVER 5 1/2" RIGID INSULATION OVER 1/4" METAL DECKING OVER 1'-4" METAL BAR JOIST.

T.O. ROOF
15' - 0"

TOP OF GYP. BD.

2' X 4' ACOUSTIC CEILING TILES.

1' - 0"

CEILING
10' - 0"

5/8" GYP. BD. OVER 7/8" METAL FURRING.

WINDOW OPENING

FIXED WINDOW 36" X 48".

4' - 0"

4" CONCRETE FLOOR SLAB OVER 2" SAND w/6"X6" #4 REIN.

3' - 0"

CONCRETE WALKWAY.

FIRST FLOOR
0' - 0"

T.O. FOOTER
-1' - 0"

CONCRETE FOOTER. SEE DETAIL FOR SIZES.

Wall Section Annotation

9. When adding the notes and dimensions:
   - Click on the Edit Type button.
   - Click on the Duplicate.
   - Create a new linear dimension style based on the Linear - 3/32" Arial style.
   - Name the new style:
     Linear - 3/32" Arial (Inches Only).
   - This style is to be used for the 8" dimension on the Eyebrow location dimension and the dimensions less than 1'-0" in length on the Exterior Bearing Footer.

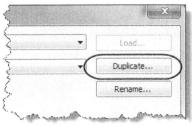

Duplicate... Button

10. Scroll down to the Units Format Parameter and click the button to the right.

Units Format Parameter

11. Check the Suppress 0 feet checkbox.

Supress 0 feet Checkbox

12. When adding the Break Lines:
   - Use the edge of the crop region as a guide.
   - Press the Spacebar to rotate the Break Line.
   - Use the arrows to adjust the size of the break and the location of the top and bottom lengths.

Break Line

13. Copy the Break Line up the side of the view.
    - Stretch the line ends until they join.
    - Continue the copies until you have four break lines.

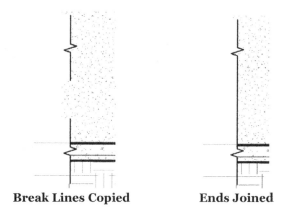

Break Lines Copied   **Ends Joined**

Creating the Exterior Bearing Detail

1. After completing the Wall Section annotations, use the Callout tool to create a detail view of the footer.

2. Detail Callout boundary placed.
    - Name the new detail: EXTERIOR BEARING DETAIL.

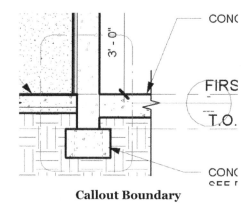

Callout Boundary

3. Double-click on the bubble to open.

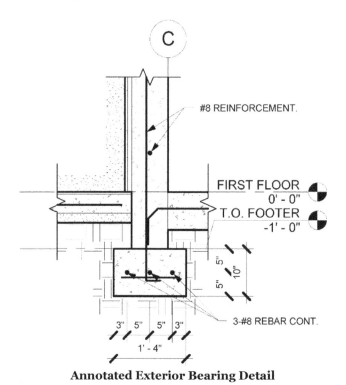

Annotated Exterior Bearing Detail

4. When placing the rebar ends, use the Filled Region tool.
   - Set the region Solid Black.
   - Use the Circle option in the Draw panel to draw the shape.
   - The radius is 1/2".

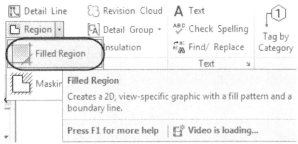
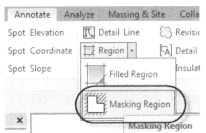

Filled Region Tool

5. When placing the lines for the rebar, use the Detail Line tool, Medium Lines style. Estimate the location based off the drawing.

6. To mask out a portion of the patterning:
   - Click on the Masking Region tool in the Annotate ribbon, Detail panel.
   - Set the linestyle of the boundary to Invisible Lines. This way the boundary will not show.
   - Draw a rectangular shape for the portion of the patterning that you wish to mask out.
   - Click the Green Check to finish.
   - Create two more regions at the top left and bottom right corners of the detail.

Masking Region Tool

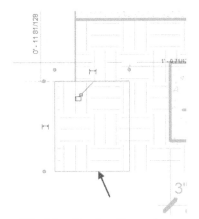

Masking Region Boundary

7. This is the end of Part 4. Save your file as CL6-4.

CL6-5 - Setting Up the Design Option Views

Next you will set up the four views that show the different design option combinations. Since there are a total of four options, you will need four views.

1. Continuing from the CL6-4 file, save the file as CL6-5.

2. In the 3D view, right-click on the view in the project browser and select Duplicate View, Duplicate.

3. The new view opens. Hide the topography.

4. Rotate the view so that you can clearly see the tower walls and roof.

5. Before duplicating the view again, reset the home position of the view.

    - Hover over the ViewCube so that the Home icon appears.

Home Icon

6. Right-click on the icon.
    - Select: Set Current View as Home
    - This will place this view rotation in memory so that you will be able to return to it if you need to rotate the view.

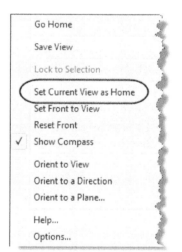

Set Current View as Home

7. Name the view: Design Option – Wall 1, Roof 1

8. Repeat the process to create three more views. Refer to the Project Browser screenshot for the names.

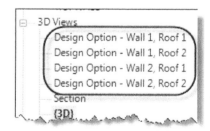

View Names for Design Options

9. Open the Visibility/Graphics Overrides dialog box by typing VV on the keyboard.
   - In the dialog box, click on the Design Options tab.
   - Refer to the table for the setup.

View Name	Design Option	
	Tower Wall Option	Tower Roof Option
Design Option – Wall 1, Roof 1	1 – Arched Opening (Primary)	1 – Flat Roof (Primary)
Design Option – Wall 1, Roof 2	1 – Arched Opening (Primary)	2 – Hip Roof
Design Option – Wall 2, Roof 1	2 – Rectangular Opening	1 – Flat Roof (Primary)
Design Option – Wall 2, Roof 2	2 – Rectangular Opening	2 – Hip Roof

Design Option Settings for Views

10. Later you will set up a sheet in the Portfolio that will show these four views.

11. This is the end of Part 5 and Tutorial 6. Save your file as CL6-5.

Tutorial 7 – Adding Additional Site Elements and Creating the Renderings	
Part 1	Applying Materials to the Walls and Walkway
Part 2	Adding Additional Elements to the Project
Part 3	Setting Up the Camera Views
Part 4	Setting up the Sky Background

CL7-1 - Applying Materials to the Walls and Walkway

The following procedures will help you to set up the exterior view of the structure. These procedures will cover materials, backgrounds, and additional site elements.

You will need to setup the materials for the exterior surface of the walls, walkways, and parking lot. Use these settings to set the correct materials.

1. Open the drawing file from Tutorial 6 named CL6-5. Save the file as CL7-1.

2. Open the Material Browser dialog box.

3. Right click on the "Concrete, Cast-in-Place gray" material and duplicate it. Name the new material Concrete, Cast-in-Place – Formwork Holes (2' Spacing).

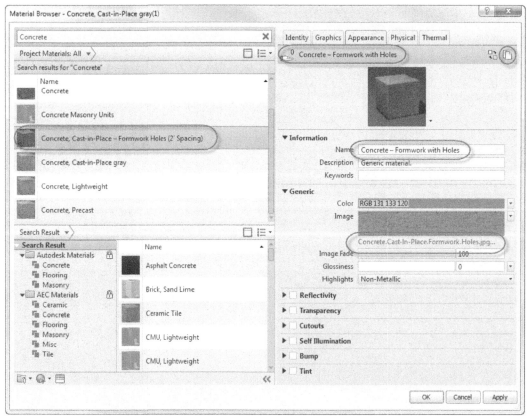

Material Browser Setting for Exterior Wall Material

4. Click on the Appearance Tab.

5. In the Assets area under tabs, click on the two white papers to the right. This will duplicate the asset.

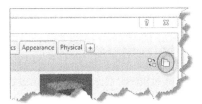

Duplicates this asset. Button

6. Click the arrow next to the Information area. Rename the asset Concrete – Formwork with Holes.

7. Click on the filename in the area beneath the image. Change the image file to: Concrete.Cast-In-Place.Formwork.Holes.

8. Click on the image sample to open the Texture Editor dialog box.

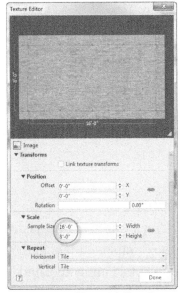

Texture Editor Dialog Box

9. Change the scale setting to 16'-0" for the Width and 8'-0" for the Height. This will space the holes 2'-0" in both directions. Click the Done button to close the box.

10. Click OK in the Material Browser to save the settings and close the box.

11. Repeat the process to create the Concrete, Walkway material. Use these settings:
    - Asset Name: Concrete Walkway
    - Image File: Concrete.Cast-In-Place.Flat.Polished.Grey
    - Scale: 16'-0" Width, 16'-0" Height

12. For the Tower walls the exterior and interior face use the Stucco material. Open the Material Browser and set the Stucco material to the following settings:
    - Surface Pattern: Gypsum-Plaster
    - Tint Color: RGB 109 100 82 (or you may choose your own color)

13. This is the end of Part 1. Save your file as CL7-1.

CL7-2 - Adding Additional Elements to the Project

To add realism to your project you may choose to add additional site elements to your project. To add people, cars, and parking stalls follow the procedure.

1. Continuing from the CL7-1 file, save the file and then save the file again as CL7-2.

2. Click on the edge of the topography and click the Edit Surface tool in the contextual tab.

3. Pull the four points away from the edge of the building as shown. (The exact distance is not important.)

Relocated Points

4. Click the Green Check to finish editing the topography.

5. Click on the Component tool in the Architecture tab, Build panel.

6. Click on the Load Family tool and load the following families: (All of the families are located in the Entourage folder.)

    - RPC Male
    - RPC Female
    - RPC Beetle
    - Van

7. Open the First Floor view.

8. Place two people near the front entrance as shown.

    - The arrow on the family indicates the direction the person is facing.

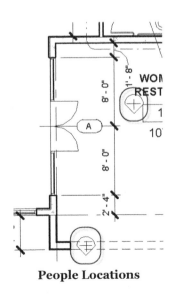

People Locations

9. Click on the Parking Component tool in the Massing & Site tab, Model Site panel.

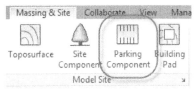

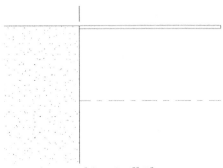

Parking Component Tool

10. Place a parking stall at the top right corner of the concrete walkway as shown.
    - When placing, set the offset to -0'-6" in the properties box.

First Parking Stall Placement

11. Click on the stall and then select the Array tool.
    - Set the Number: setting to 8 and the Move To: to 2nd.

12. Click the second point 9'-0" in a downward direction.

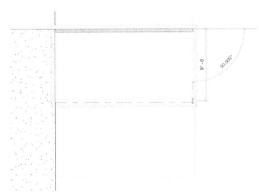

Selecting Direction of Array and Spacing

13. Eight parking stalls are created. Add the
    two vehicles as shown.

    • Add additional parking on the south
      side of the building.

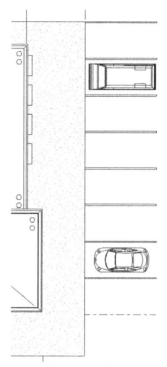

Parking Stalls Added with Vehicles

14. After you have added the parking stalls,
    you may turn off the dashed reference for
    the family.

    • Type VV to open the Visibility/Graphics
      Overrides Dialog.

    • In the Visibility column, scroll down to
      Parking.

    • Uncheck the box next to the Reference Line
      subcategory.

Reference Line Subcategory

Adding the Window Shading (Eyebrows)

Next, you will also add window shading (also known as eyebrows) above the windows and doors. After that, you will add two block walls on the north and west side of the building.

1. Open the East Elevation View.

2. Zoom in on the four windows.

3. Go to the Component Model In-place tool.

4. Pick Generic Models for the Family Category.

5. Name the Family, Eyebrow 1.

6. The view will turn gray. Set the work place to the wall facing you. You may need to mouse over the edge and press the Tab key until the wall highlights.

7. Pick the Extrusion tool in the Forms panel.

Extrusion Tool

8. Draw the shape above the left window opening as shown in the diagram.

   - After drawing the shape, dimension and lock the 8" and 4" sizes.

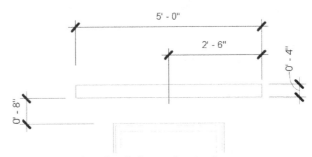

Sketch of Shape for Eyebrow

9. Set the extrusion distance to 1'-6".

10. Set the material to Concrete, Cast-in-Place, Gray

11. Click the green check to complete the component. Click the green check one more time to finish the model.

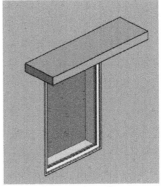

3D View of Eyebrow

12. Copy the component three times to place over the other windows.

13. To copy the component to the other windows and doors, switch to the first floor view. Use the center of the windows as the start point of the copy and endpoints of the copy.

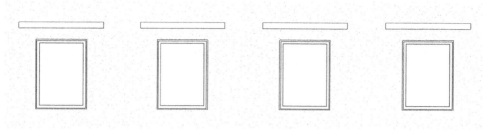

Eyebrows Copied

14. Switch to the Roof Plan view.

15. Use the Copy tool to copy the one of the components from the east wall to the north wall.

Eyebrow Copied from East Elevation

16. After copying, rotate the component 90 degrees and align the edge to the wall face. You will need to temporarily hide the coping to see the wall face.

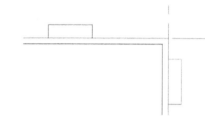

Eyebrow Rotated and Aligned to Wall Face

17. Unhide the coping and switch to the North Elevation view.

18. Adjust the location of the first eyebrow and then copy five times to each window.

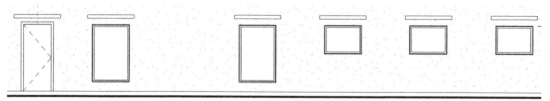

North Elevation Eyebrows Located

19. Copy the component five times to place over the windows.

20. Repeat the process one more time for the single window on the west side of the building.

Create a new component for the Curtain Wall on the south side.

21. Open the South Elevation view. Zoom in on the Curtain Wall area.

22. Click the Component Model In-Place tool.

23. Pick the south wall for the reference plane.

24. Draw the shape as shown in the diagram. Note that the thickness is now 6".

Curtain Wall Eyebrow

25. Set the extrusion distance to 3'-0".

26. Click the green check to complete the component.

Adding the Block Walls

1. Switch to the Site Plan View.

2. Add two walls. Use these settings:
   - Wall Type: Generic – 8" Masonry
   - Base Constraint: FIRST FLOOR
   - Base Offset: -0'-6"
   - Top Constraint: Unconnected
   - Unconnected Height: 6'-0"

3. Place the two walls 100'-0" from the north and west edges of the building as shown.

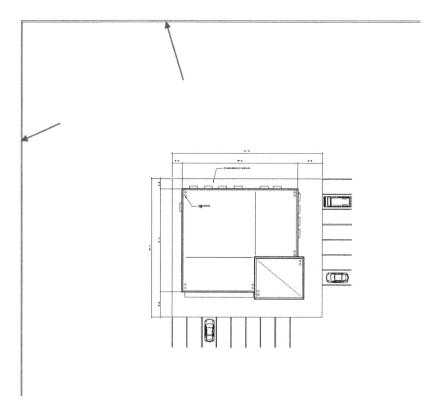

Masonry Walls Placed

4. This completes the building elements.

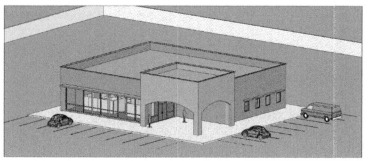

Exterior View

5. This is the end of Part 2. Save your file as CL7-2.

CL7-3 - Setting Up the Camera Views

In this part, you will create the camera views and renderings. There are two methods that you may use to create the renderings. The first method is to render the views using the Revit program and your computer. When using this method you will use Medium for the quality settings. You may wish to set the quality to Draft when checking the materials and lighting. The rendered views do not need to match exactly with the examples. Use this chart for recommended rendering settings.

View Name	Lighting Scheme
Cubicle Area	Interior: Sun and Artificial
Exterior View	Exterior: Sun and Artificial
Lobby	Exterior: Sun and Artificial
Office	Interior: Sun and Artificial
Section	Exterior: Sun and Artificial

Notes:
- Rendering times can vary from a few minutes to an hour. To save time, you may use multiple computers (if available) to render the various views.
- Rendering times may be shortened by reducing the number of lights that are turned on. This can be adjusted by using the Artificial Lights... button in the Rendering dialog box.
- Once the rendering is complete, export the rendering as a separate file to your folder.

The second method is to use the Cloud Rendering website provided by Autodesk. This will allow you to render your project on their website rather than using your own computer. Not only is this method quicker (approx. 30 times faster) but it will not tie up your computer while you file is rendered.

To use this free service, you will need to have Autodesk Student Community account. If you do not have an account and are a current college or high school student you may visit the Autodesk website to create one. If you are not a current student, you may sign up at the Autodesk 360 site for a free trial.

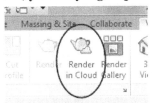

Render in Cloud Tool

Once the rendering is complete you may insert the file onto your sheet either by dragging and dropping the rendering from your project browser or by inserting the file from the folder on your drive.

Completed Rendering with Site Elements

1. Continuing from the CL7-2 file, save the file and then save the file again as CL7-3.

2. Open the First Floor Plan – Furniture view.

3. Start by creating a camera view for the Cubicle Area. Zoom in on the Lobby/Cubicles area.

4. Click on the 3D View tool in the View ribbon, Create panel. Select the Camera tool.

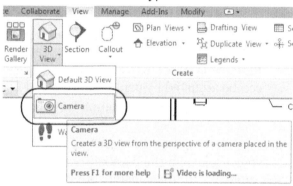

Camera Tool

5. Click a point for the camera and drag through the area.

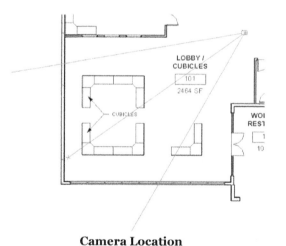

Camera Location

6. Adjust the window to match the example shown.

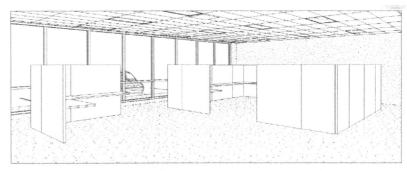

Cubicle Camera View

7. Repeat the process for the Office and Lobby.

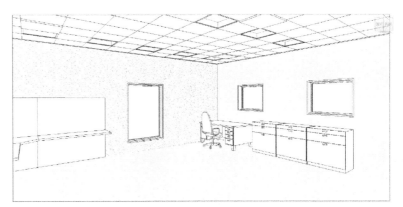

Lobby Camera View

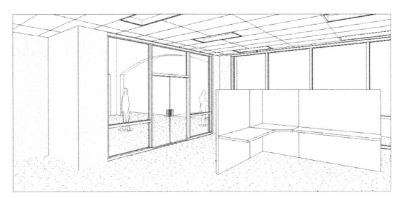

Office Camera View

8. For the section view, you will need to create a 3d section view.

- Open a 3D view.
- In the Properties Palette, click the Section Box checkbox.
- Drag the one of the Control Arrows into the building.

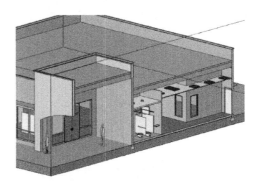

3D Section View

9. Open the Site Plan view. For the exterior view, position the camera at the lower left corner of the building as shown.

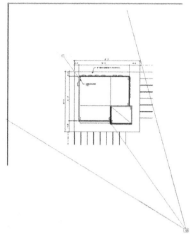

Camera Location for Exterior View

10. Adjust the window and rotation. Turn on the shadow toggle and adjust the sun angle.

    - For this view the azimuth was set to 135° and the altitude was set to 20°.

Exterior View with Shadows

11. This is the end of Part 3. Save your file as CL7-3.

CL7-4 - Setting up the Sky Background

You may either use the sky background that comes with the software or use a custom image. This procedure will cover using a custom image for the background of your project.

1. Continuing from the CL7-3 file, save the file and then save the file again as CL7-4.

2. Click on the Render tool in the View tab, Graphics panel.

3. In the Rendering Dialog box...
   - In the Style pulldown, select Image.
   - Click on the Customize Image... button.

Rendering Dialog Box

4. In the Background Image dialog box, click on the Image... button and select the Sky Background.jpg file from your Families folder.

   Click the Stretch button to fit the image to the window.

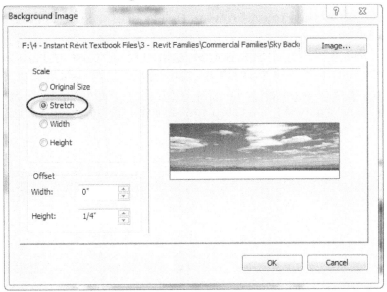

Background Image Dialog Box

5. Adjust the settings so that the background image is positioned correctly depending on the camera position for your project.

6. You must render the view to see the background image. (It may take a few tries to position the image correctly.)

7. This is the end of Part 4 and Tutorial 7. Save your file as CL7-4.

Tutorial 8 – Assembling the Construction Documents and Portfolio

Part 1	Sheet A100	TITLE SHEET
Part 2	Sheet A101	SITE PLAN
Part 3	Sheet A102	FLOOR PLAN
		Inserting the Schedules
Part 4	Sheet A103	REFLECTED CEILING PLAN
Part 5	Sheet A104	COLOR LEGEND & FURNITURE PLAN
Part 6	Sheet A201	EAST/NORTH ELEVATIONS
	Sheet A202	SOUTH/WEST ELEVATIONS
Part 7	Sheet A301	SECT., CALLOUT, & INT. ELEVS. (Section, Floor Plan Callout, & Interior Elevations)
Part 8	Sheet A400	DESIGN OPTIONS
Part 9	Sheet A401	RENDERINGS
Part 10	Assembling the PDF Portfolio	

Starting the Tutorial

1. Open the drawing file from Tutorial 7 named CL7-4.

2. Save the file as CL8-1.

At this point you have finished creating the Model Elements for the project. All that remains is to assemble these elements into a set of sheets. In addition, not all of the views have been created. You will need to create these as well.

Before beginning the process of setting up the sheets do the following:

1. Go to the Sheets category of the Project Browser. Delete all of the sheets that came with the template file.

2. Load the modified version of the "C" Size Border located in the Custom Families folder on the website. The name of the file is C 18 x 24 Horizontal – Instant Revit!.rfa.

3. You will need to save the file at the end of each part. If this is using up too much space on your flash drive/hard drive, you may skip this step and save the file at the end of this tutorial.

CL8-1 - Sheet A100 – Title Sheet

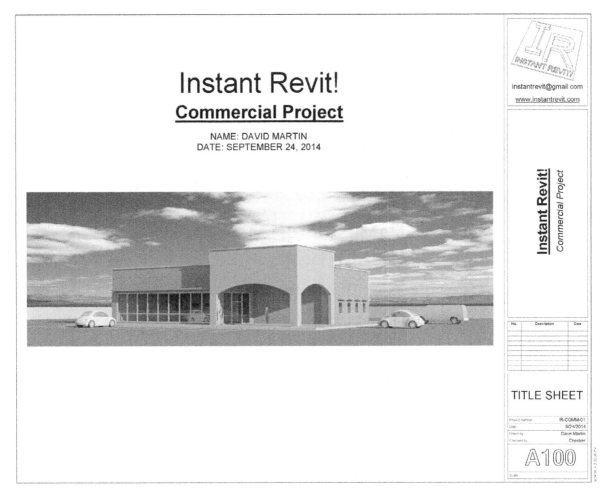

Title Sheet

1. Begin by creating the first sheet in the set. Name the sheet A100 – Title Sheet.

Sheet Title Dialog Box

2. Add the text below to the top portion of the sheet. You may need to create additional text types.
   - Use 3/4" Arial for the Instant Revit Text.
   - Use 1/2" Arial for the Commercial Project text.
   - Use 1/4" Arial for the Your Name and Date.

Instant Revit!

Commercial Project

NAME: DAVID MARTIN
DATE: SEPTEMBER 24, 2014

Text for Title Sheet

3. At the end of the Project you will create a Sheet Index and insert it onto this sheet.
4. This is the end of Part 1. Save your file as CL8-1.

CL8-2 - Sheet A101 – Site Plan

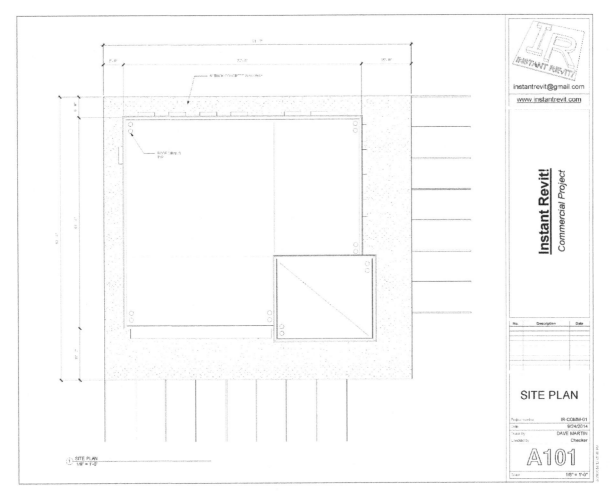

Site Plan Sheet

1. Continuing from the CL8-1 file, save the file and then save the file again as CL8-2.

2. Create a sheet named A101 – Site Plan.

3. With the sheet open, drag and drop the Site Plan view from the Floor Plans category onto the sheet. The scale is 1/8" = 1'-0". You may need to crop the view to fit it within the border.

4. This is the end of Part 2. Save your file as CL8-2.

CL8-3 - Sheet A102 – Floor Plan

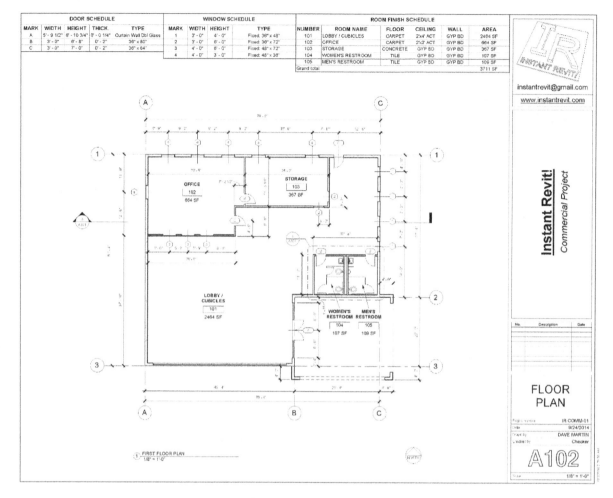

Floor Plan Sheet

1. Continuing from the CL8-2 file, save the file and then save the file again as CL8-3.

2. Create a sheet named A101 – Floor Plan.

3. With the sheet open, drag and drop the view from the Floor Plans category onto the sheet. The scale is 1/8" = 1'-0".

Inserting the Schedules

1. With the A101 sheet still open drag and drop the Door Schedule, Window Schedule, and Room Finish Schedule.

2. Re-size the width of the schedule columns to make the schedules fix exactly along the top edge of the border.

DOOR SCHEDULE					WINDOW SCHEDULE				ROOM FINISH SCHEDULE					
MARK	WIDTH	HEIGHT	THICK.	TYPE	MARK	WIDTH	HEIGHT	TYPE	NUMBER	ROOM NAME	FLOOR	CEILING	WALL	AREA
A	5'- 9 1/2"	6'- 10 3/4"	0'- 0 1/4"	Curtain Wall Dbl Glass	1	3'- 0"	4'- 0"	Fixed: 36" x 48"	101	LOBBY / CUBICLES	CARPET	2'x4' ACT	GYP BD	2464 SF
B	3'- 0"	6'- 8"	0'- 2"	36" x 80"	2	3'- 0"	6'- 0"	Fixed: 36" x 72"	102	OFFICE	CARPET	2'x2' ACT	GYP BD	664 SF
C	3'- 0"	7'- 0"	0'- 2"	36" x 84"	3	4'- 0"	6'- 0"	Fixed: 48" x 72"	103	STORAGE	CONCRETE	GYP BD	GYP BD	367 SF
					4	4'- 0"	3'- 0"	Fixed: 48" x 36"	104	WOMEN'S RESTROOM	TILE	GYP BD	GYP BD	107 SF
									105	MEN'S RESTROOM	TILE	GYP BD	GYP BD	109 SF
									Grand total					3711 SF

Schedules Located Along Top Border

3. This is the end of Part 3. Save your file as CL8-3.

CL8-4 - Sheet A103 – Reflected Ceiling Plan

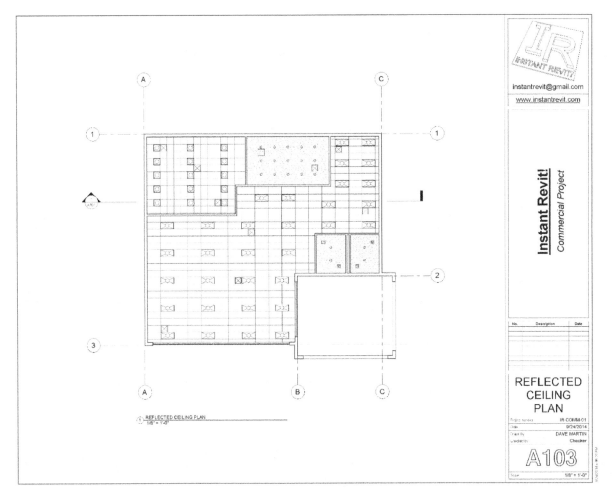

Reflected Ceiling Plan Sheet

1. Continuing from the CL8-3 file, save the file and then save the file again as CL8-4.

2. Create a sheet named A103 – Reflected Ceiling Plan.

3. With the sheet open, drag and drop the view from the Floor Plans category onto the sheet. The scale is 1/8" = 1'-0".

4. Hide the eyebrows over the door and windows to avoid confusion.

5. This is the end of Part 4. Save your file as CL8-4.

CL8-5 - Sheet A104 – Color Legend & Furniture Plan

Color Legend and Furniture Plan Sheet

1. Continuing from the CL8-4 file, save the file and then save the file again as CL8-5.

2. Create a sheet named A104 – Color Legend & Furniture Plan.

3. This sheet will contain two views on the sheet. Use 3/32" = 1'-0" for both views.

4. Drag and drop the two views onto your sheet. Align the views horizontally and center on the sheet as shown.

5. This is the end of Part 5. Save your file as CL8-5.

CL8-6 - Sheets A201 & A202 – Elevations

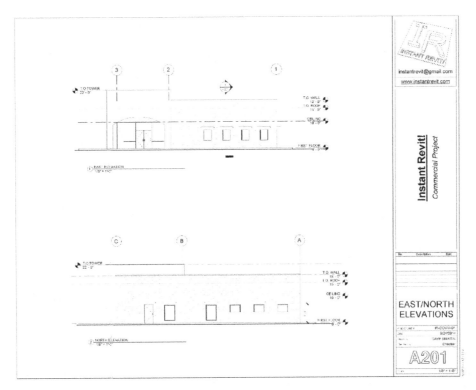

East/North Elevations

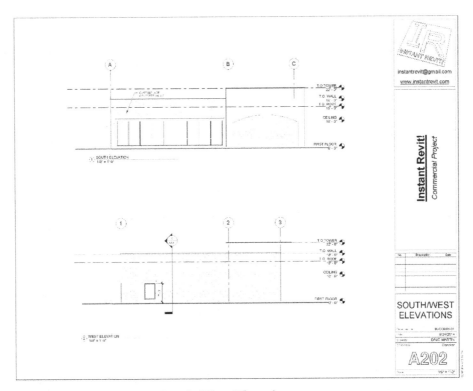

South/West Elevations

1. Continuing from the CL8-5 file, save the file and then save the file again as CL8-6.
2. Create two sheets named A201 – East/North Elevations and A202 – South/West Elevations.
3. The scale for the four elevations is 1/8" = 1'-0".
4. Drag the views onto the sheets as shown.
5. Crop the views so that the concrete walkway is visible but not the foundation.
6. This is the end of Part 6. Save your file as CL8-6.

CL8-7 - Sheet A301 – Section & Interior Elevations

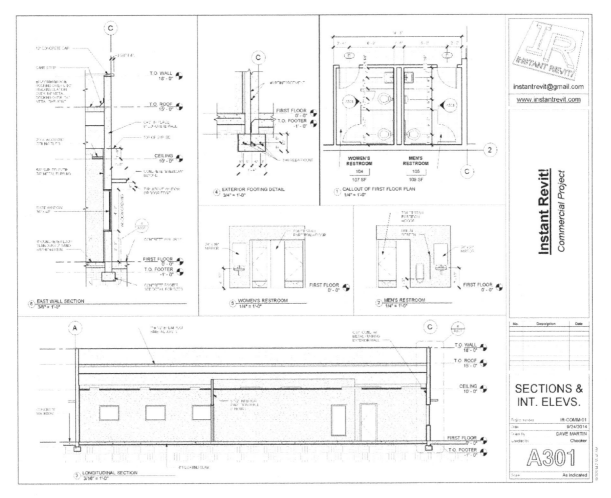

Section & Interior Elevations Sheet

1. Continuing from the CL8-6 file, save the file and then save the file again as CL8-7.

2. Create a sheet named A301 – Section & Interior Elevations.

3. Drag and drop the view named Callout of First Floor Plan onto the sheet.

4. Place the view at the upper right corner of the sheet. The scale of the view is 1/4" = 1'-0".

5. Insert the Longitudinal Section view created in Tutorial 1.

6. Drag the views of the restrooms to the appropriate locations on the sheet.

7. Insert the East Wall Section view at the upper left corner of the sheet.

8. Insert the Exterior Footing Detail between the wall section and callout views.

9. Re-number the views so as shown. Since you cannot have two views with the same number, you may need to place a letter after the number temporarily.

10. Use the Detail Line tool to add the frames around each of the views. Use the Medium Lines style.

11. This is the end of Part 7. Save your file as CL8-7.

CL8-8 - Setting Up Sheet A400 – DESIGN OPTIONS

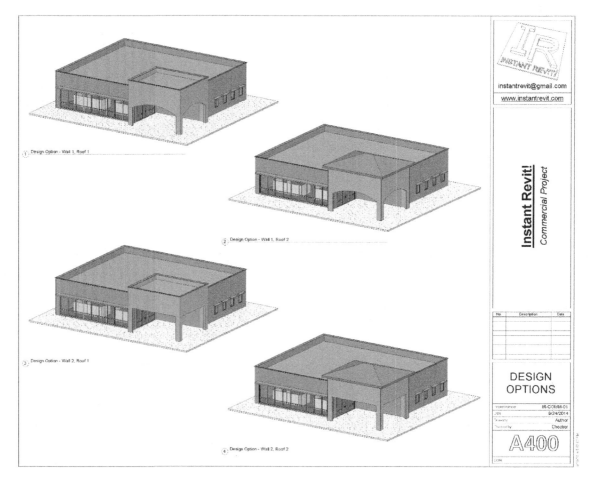

Design Options Sheet

1. Continuing from the CL8-8 file, save the file and then save the file again as CL8-9.

2. Create a sheet named A400 – DESIGN OPTIONS.

3. Go to each of the Design Option 3D views and set the scale of the view to a custom scale. You will use 1:150 for the scale.

    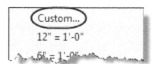

    Custom... Setting

    - Click on the View Scale setting at the bottom left of the view window.

    - Select Custom at the top of the list.

    - Set the custom scale to 1:150.

    Scale Set to 1:150

4. Return to the sheet view and drag and drop the views onto the sheet. Arrange as shown in the example.

5. This is the end of Part 8. Save your file as CL8-8.

CL8-9 - Setting Up Sheet A401 – RENDERINGS

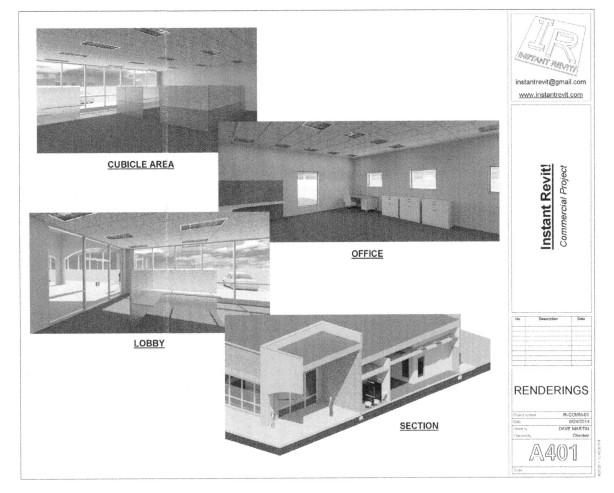

Renderings Sheet

6. Continuing from the CL8-8 file, save the file and then save the file again as CL8-9.

7. Create a sheet named A400 -- RENDERINGS.

8. Go to the Insert tab, Import panel, Image tool to insert the images. You may also drag and drop the renderings from the Renderings category if you used the Revit program to create your renderings.

9. Use the handles on the corners to size the images.

10. Use the text tool to create captions for the views. The size of the text is 1/4".

11. Insert the Exterior View rendering onto your A100 sheet.

Notes:
- You may position the images in any location that you wish.
- If you wish to crop the images you will need to use a bitmap editing program.

12. This is the end of Part 9. Save your file as CL8-9.

CL8-10 - Assembling the PDF Portfolio

1. Continuing from the CL8-9 file, save the file and then save the file again as CL8-10.

2. Now that you have finished creating the sheets, you will create a Sheet Index. Follow this procedure to create the index.

- Go to the Schedules tool and select the Sheet List Tool.

Sheet List Tool

- In the Sheet List Properties, add the Sheet Number and Sheet Name fields.

- Add a new Parameter called Sheet Order.

  Use Number for the Type of Parameter.

Sheet Order Parameter

- Setup the fields as shown...

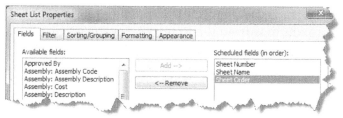

Sheet List Fields

- Set the font sizes using the Appearance tab and the Font tool in the appearance panel.
  i)   For the Title of the Sheet Index use Arial Black, 1/4", Bold, Underline.
  ii) For the header text use Arial, 9/64", Underline.
  iii) For the body text use Arial, 1/8".
  iv) Sort the schedule by the Sheet Order. After sorting hide the column.

• Setup the columns as shown...

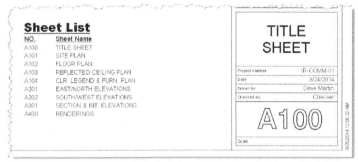

Sheet Index Set Up

3. When finished setting up the Sheet Index, drag the schedule onto the Title Sheet in the lower right corner.

Sheet Index Placed

Next you will create a PDF portfolio of your project. As you did with the individual projects, you will use the PDF ReDirect v2 program to create the PDF files of each sheet and merge them into one file.

If you are working at home, you may download the program at www.exp-systems.com.

4. Click on the Application Menu and select the Print command.

Print Command

5. The Print dialog box opens. Match the settings as shown.

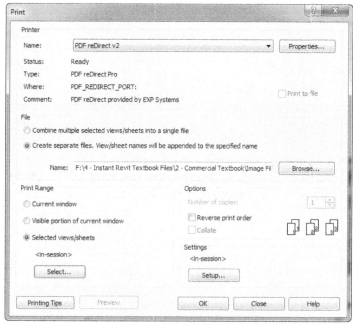

Print Dialog Box

6. Click on the Select... button in the Print Range area.

Select... Button

7. The View/Sheet Set dialog opens. Uncheck the Views checkbox and select the sheets as shown. Click the OK button.

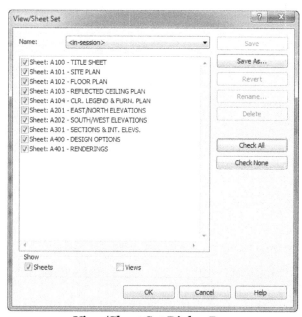

View/Sheet Set Dialog Box

8. Click the Setup... button at the bottom
right corner of the dialog box.

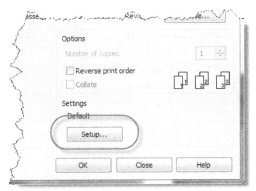

Setup... Button

9. Match the settings in the Print Setup
dialog as shown...

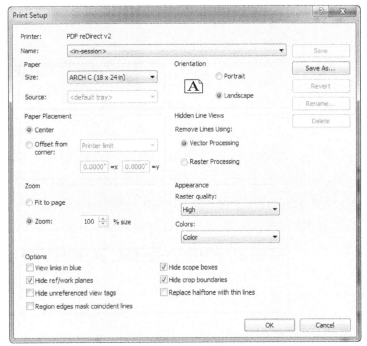

Print Setup Dialog

10. Click the OK button to close the dialog box. Click OK in the Print dialog to begin creating the PDF files. It will take a few minutes as each file is created.

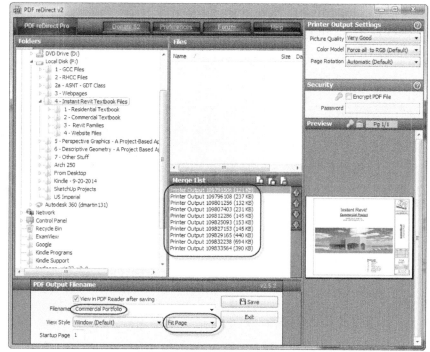

PDF ReDirect v2 Interface

11. Name the file Commercial Portfolio.pdf and set the View Style to Fit page.

12. Once completed you will have nine sheets.

13. This is the end of Part 10, Tutorial 8, and the Commercial Project. Save your file as RL8-10.

Congratulations on Completing the Commercial Project!

Glossary of Terms and Tools

Note: All screenshots are from the Autodesk® Revit® software.

Add-Ins	Programs that may be added to be used within the Revit® software.
Align(ed)	Elements that line up with one another. The Align tool in the Modify ribbon is used for this. Also used for the Aligned Dimension dimension style.
Annotation(s)	Elements such as: text, dimensions, or symbols that are placed in 2D or 3D views.
Application Menu	By clicking on the Revit Icon in the upper left corner of the screen you can open the Application menu. This will allow you to perform various tasks such as: Save, Open, and Print.
Autodesk®	The company the makes the Revit® software.
Callout	A portion of the view that shown in a separate view at a finer scale to show more detail. The tool is located in the View ribbon.

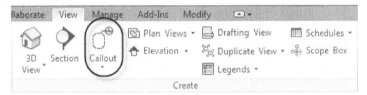

Callout Tool

Camera View	A three dimension view of that structure that is in perspective projection. The view is created by using the Camera tool in the 3D View tool located in the Create Panel, View Ribbon.
Cascade (Windows)	Arranging and opening views/windows so that all they are of equal size and overlapping one another.
Component	This tool is used to add an existing family or create a Model in the project using the Model In-Place option.
Contextual Tab	A tab on the ribbon that appears while using a particular tool. Contains tools that are specific to the current command. The tab is green in color and will disappear when the command is completed.

**Contextual Tab
(Place Door Tab Shown)**

Core	The inner portion of an element. Usually is used as structural support. Example: The structural core of a wall.
Curtain Wall	A type of wall that does not provide support for the structure. Usually made of glass panels with mullions.

Near the Application Menu description:

**Application
Menu Icon**

Curtain Grid	Used with Curtain Wall elements. A curtain grid is a system of lines that is used to separate a larger panel. These are required to add mullions to a curtain wall.
Cut (Geometry)	To remove material where two elements intersect. Located in the Modify ribbon.

Cut Tool

Cut Plane	This is a portion of the plan view that is visible in section. By default this is set to 4'-0" above the floor level but may be raised or lowered depending on the desired result. This setting is changed in the Properties Palette in the View Range setting.
Datum	A base or reference surface than provides a location reference for other elements. An example would be the first floor line on an elevation view. This height would be set to zero and other heights in the project would be measured from it.
Design Options	Allows the user to create different designs of the project within the same Revit file. Located in the Manage ribbon.

Design Options Tool

Detail	Elements that are placed in two dimensional views. A detail line would only be visible in the view in which it was placed. A level is a type of datum.
Detail Level	The level of detail that is shown in the view. The settings are: course, medium, and fine. This is adjusted at the bottom of the screen in the View Control Bar.

Detail Level Tool

Drafting View	A two-dimensional view. May be used for structural details or other annotative elements.
Dormer	An opening created in a sloped roof for an additional roof structure.
Element	A single object within the project. A line of text would be considered a text element.
Export	To take elements from the file (or the entire file) and convert them to another format so that it may be opened in a different application. The Export tool is located in the Application Menu.
Extrusion	When a flat shape is extended (or extruded) into a solid. This method of creating elements is used in the Roof tool, Modeling components, Slab edges, etc...

Face	The outside surface or edge of an element. The Face of Core option may be used when placing dimensions to locate wall locations.
Family(ies)	A single element or collection of Revit elements that may be added to the project as a group. Examples include doors, windows, and cabinetry. These files have the .rfa file extension.
Footprint	An area or shape that is created to define the size and shape of an element such as a floor or roof. This is done while in Sketch Mode. The lines that make up the edge of the footprint are magenta in color.
Grid(s)	Lines that are added to the project to aid in locating walls or columns. Usually used on larger or commercial projects. The Grid tool is located in the Datum panel in the Architecture tab. Grids may also refer to lines that divide a curtain wall.
Group	A collection of elements that are made part of a single group. This is done so that the group of elements may be modified as one. Located in the Modify ribbon.

Create Group Tool

GUI	Graphics User Interface. The interface of the Revit program.
Host	An element that provides a place for another component to become a part of it. A Stair would be considered a host for the railings.
Import	To bring in elements from another file.
Info Center	Used to access the help file, sign in to Autodesk 360, and access other resources.

Info Center

Join (Geometry)	To merge two elements together to eliminate seam lines. Located in the Modify ribbon.

Join Tool

Legend	A key that defines the meaning of diagrams or notes. The tool is located within the Create panel in the View tab. A legend would be used to show the meaning of electrical symbols.
Level	A key height within the project. Floor, roof, and footers may all be assigned a level within the project. Levels may also be used to generate views.
Mass	A type of three-dimensional element that can be converted to a roof, wall, or floor.
MEP	Mechanical, Electrical, and Plumbing.
Model (Elements)	A three-dimensional structure or collection of elements that are placed in a three dimensional view.

Mullion   A separator between two panels of a curtain wall. A curtain grid must be placed before adding a mullion.

Object Styles   A dialog box that sets the line weight, color, pattern and material of different categories and types of elements. Located in the Settings panel in the Manage Ribbon.

Offset   Tool used to move or copy an element in a parallel direction to the existing element at a set distance. Located in the Modify ribbon.

Offset Tool

Options Bar   This bar appears when the program needs information about a particular command. The bar will turn off when the command is ended.

Portion of the Place Wall Options Bar

Paint   A tool that is used to override a surface of an element with a different material. Located in the Modify palette.

Property Line   A line the shows the legal boundary of the property. This line is typically shown on the Site Plan view. The line may be sketched or added using distances and bearing (direction) values. The Property Line tool is located in the Massing & Site Ribbon.

Reference Plane   A three dimensional plane that is used to provide a location in the project for other elements to be anchored or dimensioned. May be used as a construction line within the project.

Quick Access Toolbar   The tool bar located at the top of the screen. Contains commonly used tools such as Open, Save, Undo, etc...

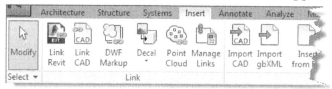

Quick Access Toolbar

Ribbon   The entire collection of panels and tools that appear when the tab is selected.

A Portion of the Insert Ribbon

Pad   A flat surface that is created as part of the topography. Provides a place for the structure on a sloped site. The Building Pad tool is in the Model Site Panel, Massing & Site ribbon is used.

Panel	A collection of tools within the Ribbon Panel.

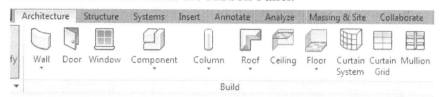

Build Panel (With the Architecture Ribbon)

Parameter	The name of an adjustable value within a family.
Phases	Also known as Phasing. Used to organize the project based on the stage of construction that the elements are a part of. An example of phases would be Existing and New Construction.
Plan Region	A portion of the plan view that has a different View Range setting as the rest of the view. This tool is located in the Create Panel in the View Ribbon.

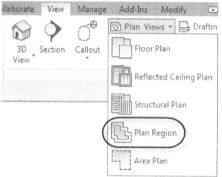

Plan Region Tool

Project Browser	Shows a tree-type view of the plan views, 3D views, elevations (exterior and interior), sections, detail views, legends, schedules, sheets, families, and groups of the project. Usually located on the left side of the screen below the Properties Palette.

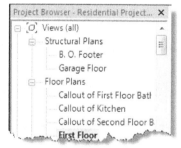

Project Browser

Properties (Type and Instance)	The parameters of an element, component, or family. Type properties affect all instances of the element within the project. Instance properties only affect one element.

Properties Palette	Contains information about the selected object. Some of the parameters may be modified.	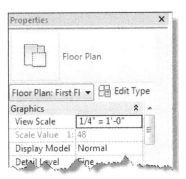

Properties Palette
(Showing Floor Plan View Properties)

PDF   Portable Document File. A file format developed by the Adobe® corporation that is used as a file format for images of Revit drawings. This format is free to use. The file has a .pdf file extension. The PDF redirect v2 program is used in the book tutorials to convert files to this format.

Purge   As in to remove (purge) unused elements from the drawing.

Raster   A type of image or output of a Revit file that consists of pixels instead of lines and shapes (vector elements). Images and shaded views are printed in this way.

Rebar   Reinforcement bar. Used to strengthen concrete slabs and walls and to reduce cracking.

Render   To convert a vector or shaded view into a raster image file. This may be done within the software or by using the Autodesk® 360 Cloud Rendering service.

Revision   A change that is made to the project. The change may be documented in a Revision Block.

Separator   Used to separate a space such as a room into two separate spaces that may be labeled separately. The Room Separator tool in the Architecture tab is used to do this.

Room Separator Tool

Schedule   A tabular element that shows information about a type of element. Doors, Windows, and Rooms may have schedules created for them. This helps to eliminate notes on the drawing by placing the information in the schedule. Schedules may be created by using the Schedules tool in the View ribbon.

Schedules Tool

Sheet	A view of the project that contains one of more view windows. Typically includes a title block. Located in the View ribbon.

Sheet Tool

Sketch & Sketch Mode	The preliminary process in creating a solid from a shape. When beginning a roof, the first step is to create a roof sketch. When the program is in sketch mode, most of the tools are grayed out and the contextual (green) tab is active. To leave sketch mode the green check or red "X" is clicked.
Sketch Path	A line that is drawn to indicate the location and length for railing element.
Slab	A flat surface with thickness. This is usually applied to floor slabs.
Snap	Assists in locking a new element to an existing element. Elements may be locked to the endpoint, midpoint, nearest, center, tangency, etc... Located in the Manage ribbon.

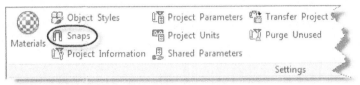

Snaps Tool

Split Face	A tool used to create separate faces on one face. Used to change the major material of a large surface such as bathroom tile with the floor of a building. Located in the Modify ribbon.

Split Face Tool

Status Bar	Gives information and prompts for the current tool and process. Located at the bottom left side of the screen.

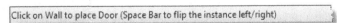

Click on Wall to place Door (Space Bar to flip the instance left/right)

Status Bar (Prompt for Door Tool Shown)

Structural	These are elements of the model that provide support. Example: Columns, Structural Walls, etc...
Subregion	A portion of the toposurface that is separate from the major region. This is done to change a portion of the toposurface to a different material. The Subregion tool is in the Model Site Panel, Massing & Site ribbon.
Switch Windows	Allows the user to switch from one open file/view to another by selecting from a list of views. Tool is located in the View ribbon.

Switch Window Tool

Tab   Located at the top of the Revit interface. By clicking on a tab the ribbon will be visible. Example: Architecture Tab (see graphic).

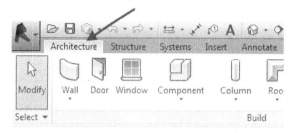

Architecture Tab

Tag   A label that is attached to a family or space such as a door, window, or room. The tag may be attached when the element is added to the projects or later in the project.

Template File   A file that is used when beginning a new drawing file. Has the extension of .rte. Example: Residential-Default.rte.

Tile (Windows)   Arrange open views/windows so that all are of equal size and completely visible.

Title Block   A portion of the border that contains information about the project. May be loaded from a title block family file or included in the template file.

Toposurface   A surface that is created when adding topography to the project. A toposurface may be created from points place in the view or from imported drawings or files.

Type Selector   Located in the Properties Box. This allows the user to select different types of elements within the same family such as: door and window types.

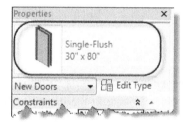

Type Selector Showing a Door Type

Vector   A type of file where the elements consist of lines and shapes instead of individual pixels. Revit construction documents are usually printed in this format.

View   A plan (top) or elevation (side) image of the object taken at a particular height or level.

View Control Bar   Shows view-related tools such as: view scale, detail level, view display, sun settings, shadow toggle, crop window settings, and temporary visibility settings.

View Control Bar

View Range   The top and bottom of the view. The view is setup so that only objects are visible that are between the upper and lower range. This is adjusted in the View Properties dialog box.

Walkthrough	A collection of rendered images that simulate traveling around or through a project.
Wall Join	A tool used to override the automatic joining of two walls.
Witness Lines	The extension line of a dimension.

Conclusion

Congratulations on Completing the Project!

You should now have an excellent understanding of the techniques required to create a one-story commercial building using the Autodesk Revit 2015 design software. Feel free to continue to modify this project with additional elements such as additional parking, exterior lighting, additional site elements, etc...

I hope that you have enjoyed the project and will recommend this book to others. Please feel free share your experiences that you have had while working through the project and also feel free to offer any suggestions to improve the book.

Once again, congratulations and good luck in your future study of Revit and Architecture!

Sincerely,

David Martin
instantrevit@gmail.com
instantrevit.com

September, 2014

Index

Made in the USA
Coppell, TX
15 January 2021

48271453R00079